MznLnx

Missing Links Exam Preps

Exam Prep for

A First Course in Abstract Algebra

Rotman, 2nd Edition

The MznLnx Exam Prep is your link from the texbook and lecture to your exams.
The MznLnx Exam Preps are unauthorized and comprehensive reviews of your textbooks.

All material provided by MznLnx and Rico Publications (c) 2010
Textbook publishers and textbook authors do not particpate in or contribute to these reviews.

MznLnx

Rico
Publications

Exam Prep for A First Course in Abstract Algebra
2nd Edition
Rotman

Publisher: Raymond Houge
Assistant Editor: Michael Rouger
Text and Cover Designer: Lisa Buckner
Marketing Manager: Sara Swagger
Project Manager, Editorial Production: Jerry Emerson
Art Director: Vernon Lowerui

Product Manager: Dave Mason
Editorial Assitant: Rachel Guzmanji
Pedagogy: Debra Long
Cover Image: Jim Reed/Getty Images
Text and Cover Printer: City Printing, Inc.
Compositor: Media Mix, Inc.

(c) 2010 Rico Publications
ALL RIGHTS RESERVED. No part of this work
covered by the copyright may be reproduced or
used in any form or by an means--graphic, electronic,
or mechanical, including photocopying, recording,
taping, Web distribution, information storage, and
retrieval systems, or in any other manner--without the
written permission of the publisher.

For more information about our products, contact us at:
Dave.Mason@RicoPublications.com

For permission to use material from this text or
product, submit a request online to:
Dave.Mason@RicoPublications.com

Printed in the United States
ISBN:

Contents

CHAPTER 1
Number Theory   1
CHAPTER 2
Groups I   14
CHAPTER 3
Commutative Rings I   31
CHAPTER 4
Goodies   50
CHAPTER 5
Groups II   60
CHAPTER 6
Commutative Rings II   68
ANSWER KEY   79

TO THE STUDENT

COMPREHENSIVE

The *MznLnx* Exam Prep series is designed to help you pass your exams. Editors at MznLnx review your textbooks and then prepare these practice exams to help you master the textbook material. Unlike study guides, workbooks, and practice tests provided by the texbook publisher and textbook authors, *MznLnx* gives you **all** of the material in each chapter in exam form, not just samples, so you can be sure to nail your exam.

MECHANICAL

The MznLnx Exam Prep series creates exams that will help you learn the subject matter as well as test you on your understanding. Each question is designed to help you master the concept. Just working through the exams, you gain an understanding of the subject--its a simple mechanical process that produces success.

INTEGRATED STUDY GUIDE AND REVIEW

MznLnx is not just a set of exams designed to test you, its also a comprehensive review of the subject content. Each exam question is also a review of the concept, making sure that you will get the answer correct without having to go to other sources of material. You learn as you go! Its the easiest way to pass an exam.

HUMOR

Studying can be tedious and dry. MznLnx's instructional design includes moderate humor within the exam questions on occassion, to break the tedium and revitalize the brain

Chapter 1. Number Theory

1. The _____ are natural numbers including 0 ' href='/wiki/0_(number)'>0, 1, 2, 3, ...) and their negatives (0, −1, −2, −3, ...). They are numbers that can be written without a fractional or decimal component, and fall within the set {...
   a. AKS primality test
   b. Abelian P-root group
   c. Integers
   d. ADE classification

2. If $A_1, A_2, ..., A_n$ are _____ square matrices over a field, then

$$(A_1 A_2 \cdots A_n)^{-1} = A_n^{-1} A_{n-1}^{-1} \cdots A_1^{-1}.$$

It becomes evident why this is the case if one attempts to find an inverse for the product of the A_is from first principles, that is, that we wish to determine B such that

$$(A_1 A_2 \cdots A_n) B = I$$

where B is the inverse matrix of the product. To remove A_1 from the product, we can then write

$$A_1^{-1}(A_1 A_2 \cdots A_n) B = A_1^{-1} I$$

which would reduce the equation to

$$(A_2 A_3 \cdots A_n) B = A_1^{-1} I.$$

Likewise, then, from

$$A_2^{-1}(A_2 A_3 \cdots A_n) B = A_2^{-1} A_1^{-1} I$$

which simplifies to

$$(A_3 A_4 \cdots A_n) B = A_2^{-1} A_1^{-1} I.$$

If one repeat the process up to A_n, the equation becomes

$$B = A_n^{-1} A_{n-1}^{-1} \cdots A_2^{-1} A_1^{-1} I$$

$$B = A_n^{-1} A_{n-1}^{-1} \cdots A_2^{-1} A_1^{-1}$$

but B is the inverse matrix, i.e. $B = (A_1 A_2 \cdots A_n)^{-1}$ so the property is established.

Chapter 1. Number Theory

Over the field of real numbers, the set of singular n-by-n matrices, considered as a subset of $R^{n \times n}$, is a null set, i.e., has Lebesgue measure zero.

a. 2-bridge knot
b. Nonsingular
c. -equivalence
d. -module

3. A _____ is a complex number whose real and imaginary part are both integers. The Gaussian integers, with ordinary addition and multiplication of complex numbers, form an integral domain, usually written as Z[i]. This domain does not have a total ordering that respects arithmetic, since it contains imaginary numbers.

a. Quadratic Gauss sums
b. Jacobi sum
c. Kummer sum
d. Gaussian integer

4. The _____ are natural numbers including 0 ' href='/wiki/0_(number)'>0, 1, 2, 3, ...) and their negatives (0, −1, −2, −3, ...). They are numbers that can be written without a fractional or decimal component, and fall within the set {...

a. ADE classification
b. AKS primality test
c. Abelian P-root group
d. Integers

5. A _____ is an expression which compares quantities relative to each other. The most common examples involve two quantities, but in theory any number of quantities can be compared. In mathematical terms, they are represented by separating each quantity with a colon, for example the _____ 2:3, which is read as the _____ 'two to three'.

a. -equivalence
b. Rational number
c. Number system
d. Ratio

6. In mathematics, especially in the area of abstract algebra known as ring theory, a _____ is a ring with 0 ≠ 1 such that ab = 0 implies that either a = 0 or b = 0 (the zero-product property.) That is, it is a nontrivial ring without left or right zero divisors. A commutative _____ is called an integral _____.

a. Subring
b. Coherent ring
c. Domain
d. Partially-ordered ring

7. In ring theory, a branch of abstract algebra, an _____ is a special subset of a ring. The _____ concept generalizes in an appropriate way some important properties of integers like 'even number' or 'multiple of 3'.

For instance, in rings one studies prime ideals instead of prime numbers, one defines coprime ideals as a generalization of coprime numbers, and one can prove a generalized Chinese remainder theorem about ideals.

a. ADE classification
b. AKS primality test
c. Augmentation ideal
d. Ideal

8. In ring theory, a branch of abstract algebra, a _____ is an ideal I in a ring R that is generated by a single element a of R.

More specifically:

- a left _____ of R is a subset of R of the form $Ra := \{ra : r \text{ in } R\}$;
- a right _____ is a subset of the form $aR := \{ar : r \text{ in } R\}$;
- a two-sided _____ is a subset of the form $RaR := \{r_1 a s_1 + \ldots + r_n a s_n : r_1, s_1, \ldots, r_n, s_n \text{ in } R\}$.

If R is a commutative ring, then the above three notions are all the same. In that case, it is common to write the ideal generated by a as (a.)

Not all ideals are principal.

a. Principal ideal
b. Radical of an ideal
c. Primitive ideal
d. Radical of an ring

9. In abstract algebra, a _____ i.e., can be generated by a single element. More generally, a principal ring is a nonzero commutative ring whose ideals are principal, although some authors (e.g., Bourbaki) refers to Principal ideal domains as principal rings. The distinction being that a principal ideal ring may have zero divisors whereas a _____ cannot.

a. Nilradical
b. Discrete valuation
c. Minimal prime
d. Principal ideal domain

10. A _____ is an n × n table filled with n different symbols in such a way that each symbol occurs exactly once in each row and exactly once in each column. Here is an example: $\begin{bmatrix} 1 & 2 & 3 \\ 2 & 3 & 1 \\ 3 & 1 & 2 \end{bmatrix}$

Latin squares occur as the multiplication tables of quasigroups. They have applications in the design of experiments and in error correcting codes.

a. Latin square
b. -module
c. -equivalence
d. 2-bridge knot

11. In elementary algebra, a _____ is a polynomial with two terms--the sum of two monomials--often bound by parenthesis or brackets when operated upon. It is the simplest kind of polynomial other than monomials.

- The _____ $a^2 - b^2$ can be factored as the product of two other binomials:

    $a^2 - b^2 = (a + b)(a - b.)$

    This is a special case of the more general formula: $$a^{n+1} - b^{n+1} = (a - b) \sum_{k=0}^{n} a^k b^{n-k}$$.

- The product of a pair of linear binomials (ax + b) and (cx + d) is:

    $(ax + b)(cx + d) = acx^2 + axd + bcx + bd$.

- A _____ raised to the nth power, represented as

    $(a + b)^n$

    can be expanded by means of the _____ theorem or, equivalently, using Pascal's triangle. Taking a simple example, the perfect square _____ $(p + q)^2$ can be found by squaring the first digit, adding twice the product of the first and second digit and finally adding the square of the second digit, to give $p^2 + 2pq + q^2$.

a. Theory of equations
b. Generalized arithmetic progression
c. Content
d. Binomial

12. In mathematics, a _____ is a constant multiplicative factor of a certain object. For example, in the expression $9x^2$, the _____ of x^2 is 9.

The object can be such things as a variable, a vector, a function, etc.

a. Vandermonde polynomial
b. Constant term
c. Tschirnhaus transformation
d. Coefficient

13. A _____ is one of the basic shapes of geometry: a polygon with three corners or vertices and three sides or edges which are line segments. A _____ with vertices A, B, and C is denoted ABC.

In Euclidean geometry any three non-collinear points determine a unique _____ and a unique plane (i.e. a two-dimensional Euclidean space.)

a. -equivalence
b. -module
c. 2-bridge knot
d. Triangle

14. The _____ is a result about congruences in number theory and its generalizations in abstract algebra.

The original form of the theorem, contained in a third-century AD book Sun Zi suanjing by Chinese mathematician Sun Tzu and later republished in a 1247 book by Qin Jiushao, the Shushu Jiuzhang (æ•,æ›,ä¹ ç« Mathematical Treatise in Nine Sections) is a statement about simultaneous congruences

Suppose n_1, n_2, â€¦, n_k are positive integers which are pairwise coprime.

a. Multiplicative group of integers modulo n
b. Chinese Remainder Theorem
c. Discrete logarithm
d. Modular arithmetic

15. In ring theory, a branch of abstract algebra, a _____ is a ring in which the multiplication operation is commutative. The study of commutative rings is called commutative algebra.

Some specific kinds of commutative rings are given with the following chain of class inclusions:

- commutative rings ⊃ integral domains ⊃ unique factorization domains ⊃ principal ideal domains ⊃ Euclidean domains ⊃ fields

A ring is a set R equipped with two binary operations, i.e. operations that combine any two elements of the ring to a third. They are called addition and multiplication and commonly denoted by '+' and '·', e.g. a + b and a · b.

a. Differential calculus over commutative algebras
b. Commutative ring
c. Nilradical
d. Going up

16. In mathematics, a _____ is a type of algebraic structure. There is some variation among mathematicians as to exactly what properties a _____ is required to have, as described in detail below. However, commonly a _____ is defined as a set together with two binary operations (usually called addition and multiplication), where each operation combines two elements to form a third element.

a. 2-bridge knot
b. -module
c. -equivalence
d. Ring

17. In mathematics, the complex numbers are an extension of the real numbers obtained by adjoining an imaginary unit, denoted i, which satisfies:

$$i^2 = -1.$$

Every _____ can be written in the form a + bi, where a and b are real numbers called the real part and the imaginary part of the _____, respectively.

Complex numbers are a field, and thus have addition, subtraction, multiplication, and division operations. These operations extend the corresponding operations on real numbers, although with a number of additional elegant and useful properties, e.g., negative real numbers can be obtained by squaring complex (imaginary) numbers.

a. 2-bridge knot
b. -module
c. -equivalence
d. Complex number

18. In mathematics, in the field of algebraic number theory, a _____ is a formal product of places of an algebraic number field. It is used to encode ramification data for abelian extensions of number field.

Let K be an algebraic number field with ring of integers R. A _____ is a formal product

$$\mathbf{m} = \prod_{\mathbf{p}} \mathbf{p}^{\nu(\mathbf{p})}$$

where p runs over all places of K, finite or infinite, the exponents v are zero except for finitely many p, for real places r we have v (r)=0 or 1 and for complex places v=0.

a. Principal ideal theorem
b. Different ideal
c. Modulus
d. Quadratic field

19. In mathematics, particularly in linear algebra and functional analysis, the _____ of a matrix or linear operator is a factorization analogous to the polar form of a nonzero complex number z

$$z = re^{i\theta}$$

where r is the absolute value of z (a positive real number), and $e^{i\theta}$ is called the complex sign of z.

The _____ of a complex matrix A is a matrix decomposition of the form

$$A = UP$$

where U is a unitary matrix and P is a positive-semidefinite Hermitian matrix. This decomposition always exists; and so long as A is invertible, it is unique, with P positive-definite.

a. Cholesky decomposition
b. Positive definite function on a group
c. Riesz-Thorin theorem
d. Polar decomposition

20. _____ is the mathematical process of putting things together. The plus sign '+' means that numbers are added together. For example, in the picture on the right, there are 3 + 2 apples--meaning three apples and two other apples--which is the same as five apples, since 3 + 2 = 5.

a. ADE classification
b. Abelian P-root group
c. AKS primality test
d. Addition

21. In mathematics, an _____ is a formula such as that for the exponential function

$$e^{x+y} = e^x \cdot e^y$$

that expresses, for a particular function f, f(x + y) in terms of f(x) and f(y.) Slightly more generally, as is the case with the trigonometric functions sin and cos, several functions may be involved; this is more apparent than real, in that case, since there cos is an algebraic function of sin (in other words, we usually take their functions both as defined on the unit circle.)

The scope of the idea of an _____ was fully explored in the nineteenth century, prompted by the discovery of the _____ for elliptic functions.

a. Algebraic cycle
b. Arithmetic group
c. Algebraic stack
d. Addition theorem

22. In mathematics, a _____ of a number x is any number which, when repeatedly multiplied by itself, eventually yields x:

$$r \times r \times \cdots \times r = x.$$

In terms of exponentiation, r is a _____ of x if

$$r^n = x$$

for some positive integer n. For example, 2 is a _____ of 16 since $2^4 = 2 \times 2 \times 2 \times 2 = 16$.

The number n is called the degree of the _____.

a. Cubic function
b. Rationalisation
c. Root
d. Difference of two squares

23. An nth _____, where n = 1,2,3,Â·Â·Â·, is a complex number, z, satisfying the equation

$$z^n = 1.$$

Second roots are called square roots, and third roots are called cube roots.

An nth _____ is primitive if

$$z^k \neq 1 \quad (k = 1, 2, 3, \ldots, n-1).$$

There are n different nth roots of unity:

$$z^k \quad (k = 1, 2, 3, \ldots, n),$$

where z is any primitive nth _____. These n roots are distributed evenly over the unit circle as can be seen in the plot on the right-hand side of the three 3rd roots of unity.

a. Root of unity
b. -equivalence
c. 2-bridge knot
d. -module

24. In mathematics, a _____ of a number x is a number r such that $r^2 = x$, or, in other words, a number r whose square (the result of multiplying the number by itself) is x.

Every non-negative real number x has a unique non-negative _____, called the principal _____, which is denoted with a radical symbol as $\sqrt{x}$, or, using exponent notation, as $x^{1/2}$. For example, the principal _____ of 9 is 3, denoted $\sqrt{9} = 3$, because $3^2 = 3 \times 3 = 9$.

a. -module
b. Square root
c. 2-bridge knot
d. -equivalence

25. The _____ of an angle is the ratio of the length of the adjacent side to the length of the hypotenuse. In our case

$$\cos A = \frac{\text{adjacent}}{\text{hypotenuse}} = \frac{b}{h}.$$

The tangent of an angle is the ratio of the length of the opposite side to the length of the adjacent side. In our case

$$\tan A = \frac{\text{opposite}}{\text{adjacent}} = \frac{a}{b}.$$

The remaining three functions are best defined using the above three functions.

a. -module
b. -equivalence
c. Cosine
d. 2-bridge knot

26. The _____ of a Lie algebra $\mathfrak{g}$ is a particular ideal of $\mathfrak{g}$.

Let $\mathfrak{g}$ be a Lie algebra. The _____ of $\mathfrak{g}$ is defined as the largest solvable ideal of $\mathfrak{g}$.

a. Garside element
b. Radical
c. Cyclically reduced word
d. Class sum

27. In mathematics, especially in elementary arithmetic, _____ is an arithmetic operation which is the inverse of multiplication.

Specifically, if c times b equals a, written:

$$c \times b = a$$

where b is not zero, then a divided by b equals c, written:

$$\frac{a}{b} = c$$

For instance,

$$\frac{6}{3} = 2$$

since

$$2 \times 3 = 6.$$

In the above expression, a is called the dividend, b the divisor and c the quotient.

   a. -equivalence
   b. 2-bridge knot
   c. -module
   d. Division

28. In linear algebra, a _____ is a set of vectors that, in a linear combination, can represent every vector in a given vector space or free module, and such that no element of the set can be represented as a linear combination of the others. In other words, a _____ is a linearly independent spanning set.
   a. Supergroup
   b. Chirality
   c. Minor
   d. Basis

29. In algebraic geometry, divisors are a generalization of codimension one subvarieties of algebraic varieties; two different generalizations are in common use, Cartier divisors and Weil divisors The concepts agree on non-singular varieties over algebraically closed fields.

A Weil _____ is a locally finite linear combination (with integral coefficients) of irreducible subvarieties of codimension one.

Chapter 1. Number Theory

a. Linear system of divisors
b. Picard group
c. Lefschetz pencil
d. Divisor

30. Informally, the _____ of two polynomials p(x) and q(x) is the 'biggest' polynomial that divides evenly into both p(x) and q(x.) The definition is modeled on the concept of the _____ of two integers. This is simply the greatest integer that divides into both of them with a remainder of zero.

   a. Descartes' rule of signs
   b. Ring of symmetric functions
   c. Coefficient
   d. Greatest common divisor

31. _____, in logic and fields that rely on it such as mathematics and philosophy, is a biconditional logical connective between statements. In that it is biconditional, the connective can be likened to the standard material conditional ('if') combined with its reverse ('only if'); hence the name. The result is that the truth of either one of the connected statements requires the truth of the other, i.e., either both statements are true, or both are false.

   a. AKS primality test
   b. ADE classification
   c. Abelian P-root group
   d. If and only if

32. In algebra, a commutative ring R is said to be _____ if any of the following equivalent conditions holds:

   1. The localization $R_\mathfrak{m}$ of R at $\mathfrak{m}$ is a valuation ring for every maximal ideal $\mathfrak{m}$ of R.
   2. For all ideals $\mathfrak{a}$, $\mathfrak{b}$, and $\mathfrak{c}$,

   $$\mathfrak{a} \cap (\mathfrak{b} + \mathfrak{c}) = (\mathfrak{a} \cap \mathfrak{b}) + (\mathfrak{a} \cap \mathfrak{c})$$

   - For all ideals $\mathfrak{a}$, $\mathfrak{b}$, and $\mathfrak{c}$,

   $$\mathfrak{a} + (\mathfrak{b} \cap \mathfrak{c}) = (\mathfrak{a} + \mathfrak{b}) \cap (\mathfrak{a} + \mathfrak{c})$$

   An _____ domain is called a Prüfer domain.

a. Ordered vector space
b. Inverse eigenvalues theorem
c. Arithmetical
d. Exchange matrix

33. In linear algebra, functional analysis and related areas of mathematics, a _____ is a function that assigns a strictly positive length or size to all vectors in a vector space, other than the zero vector. A seminorm (or pseudonorm), on the other hand, is allowed to assign zero length to some non-zero vectors.

A simple example is the 2-dimensional Euclidean space R^2 equipped with the Euclidean _____.

a. -equivalence
b. -module
c. Quasinorm
d. Norm

34. In mathematics, _____ (F_n) is the outer automorphism group of a free group on n generators. These groups play an important role in geometric group theory.

_____ (F_n) acts geometrically on a cell complex known as outer space, which can be thought of as the Teichmüller space for a bouquet of circles.

a. ADE classification
b. AKS primality test
c. Abelian P-root group
d. Out

Chapter 2. Groups I

1. In mathematics, a _____ is the direct product of two sets. The _____ is named after René Descartes, whose formulation of analytic geometry gave rise to this concept.

   Specifically, the _____ of two sets X (for example the points on an x-axis) and Y (for example the points on a y-axis), denoted X × Y, is the set of all possible ordered pairs whose first component is a member of X and whose second component is a member of Y (e.g. the whole of the x-y plane):

   $$X \times Y = \{(x,y) | x \in X \text{ and } y \in Y\}.$$

   For example, the _____ of the 13-element set of standard playing card ranks {Ace, King, Queen, Jack, 10, 9, 8, 7, 6, 5, 4, 3, 2} and the four-element set of card suits {♠, ♥, ♦, ♣} is the 52-element set of all possible playing cards {(Ace, ♠), (King, ♠), ..., (2, ♠), (Ace, ♥), ..., (3, ♣), (2, ♣)}.

   a. Pointed set
   b. Cartesian product
   c. -module
   d. -equivalence

2. A _____ is a set G closed under a binary operation · satisfying the following 3 axioms:

   - Associativity: For all a, b and c in G, (a · b) · c = a · (b · c).
   - Identity element: There exists an e∈G such that for all a in G, e · a = a · e = a.
   - Inverse element: For each a in G, there is an element b in G such that a · b = b · a = e, where e is an identity element.

   Basic examples for groups are the integers Z with addition operation, or rational numbers without zero Q{0} with multiplication. More generally, for any ring R, the units in R form a multiplicative _____ Groups include, however, much more general structures than the above.

   a. Grigorchuk group
   b. Product of group subsets
   c. Nilpotent group
   d. Group

3. In several fields of mathematics the term _____ is used with different but closely related meanings. They all relate to the notion of mapping the elements of a set to other elements of the same set, i.e., exchanging (or 'permuting') elements of a set.

   The general concept of _____ can be defined more formally in different contexts:

   In combinatorics, a _____ is usually understood to be a sequence containing each element from a finite set once, and only once.

a. Near-field
b. Rupture field
c. Binary function
d. Permutation

4. The set of all symmetry operations considered, on all objects in a set X, can be modeled as a group action g : G × X → X, where the image of g in G and x in X is written as gÂ·x. If, for some g, gÂ·x = y then x and y are said to be symmetrical to each other. For each object x, operations g for which gÂ·x = x form a group, the _____ of the object, a subgroup of G. If the _____ of x is the trivial group then x is said to be asymmetric, otherwise symmetric.

a. -module
b. -equivalence
c. 2-bridge knot
d. Symmetry group

5. In mathematics, the _____ on a set X, denoted by S_X, $\mathfrak{S}_X$ or Sym(X), is the group whose underlying set is the set of all bijective functions from X to X, in which the group operation is that of composition of functions, i.e., two such functions f and g can be composed to yield a new bijective function $f \circ g$, defined by $(f \circ g)(x) = f(g(x))$ for all x in X. Using this operation, S_X forms a group. The operation is also written as fg (and sometimes, although not here, as gf.)

Of particular importance is the _____ on the finite set

$X = \{1, ..., n\}$,

denoted by S_n.

a. Frobenius group
b. Primitive permutation group
c. Symmetric group
d. Parker vector

6. In mathematics, and in particular in group theory, a _____ is a permutation of the elements of some set X which maps the elements of some subset S to each other in a cyclic fashion, while fixing (i.e., mapping to themselves) all other elements. The set S is called the orbit of the _____.

A permutation of a set X, which is a bijective function $\sigma : X \rightarrow X$, is called a _____ if the action on X of the subgroup generated by σ has exactly one orbit with more than a single element.

a. Definition.
b. Cycle
c. Continuant
d. Nested radical

7. In abstract algebra, the _____ of a module is a measure of the module's 'size'. It is defined as the _____ of the longest ascending chain of submodules and is a generalization of the concept of dimension for vector spaces. The modules with finite _____ share many important properties with finite-dimensional vector spaces.

a. Finitely generated module
b. Morita equivalence
c. Supermodule
d. Length

8. In informal language, a _____ is a function that swaps two elements of a set. More formally, given a finite set $X = \{a_1, a_2, \ldots, a_n\}$, a _____ is a permutation (bijective function of X onto itself) f, such that there exist indices i,j such that $f(a_i) = a_j$, $f(a_j) = a_i$ and $f(a_k) = a_k$ for all other indices k. This is often denoted (in the cycle notation) as (a,b.)

For example, if X = {a,b,c,d,e}, the function σ given by

$$\sigma(a) = a$$
$$\sigma(b) = e$$
$$\sigma(c) = c$$
$$\sigma(d) = d$$
$$\sigma(e) = b$$

is a _____.

Any permutation can be expressed as the composition (product) of transpositions.

a. Rencontres number
b. Cycle notation
c. Transposition
d. Stirling numbers of the first kind

9. In mathematics, _____ or factoring is the decomposition of an object ' href='/wiki/Matrix_(mathematics)'>matrix) into a product of other objects, or factors, which when multiplied together give the original. For example, the number 15 factors into primes as 3 × 5, and the polynomial $x^2 - 4$ factors as (x − 2)(x + 2.) In all cases, a product of simpler objects is obtained.

a. -module
b. 2-bridge knot
c. -equivalence
d. Factorization

10. In its simplest meaning in mathematics and logic, an _____ is an action or procedure which produces a new value from one or more input values. There are two common types of operations: unary and binary. Unary operations involve only one value, such as negation and trigonometric functions.

a. Abelian P-root group
b. AKS primality test
c. ADE classification
d. Operation

11. The _____ is a result about congruences in number theory and its generalizations in abstract algebra.

The original form of the theorem, contained in a third-century AD book Sun Zi suanjing by Chinese mathematician Sun Tzu and later republished in a 1247 book by Qin Jiushao, the Shushu Jiuzhang (æ•¸æ›¸ä¹ ç« Mathematical Treatise in Nine Sections) is a statement about simultaneous congruences

Suppose $n_1, n_2, …, n_k$ are positive integers which are pairwise coprime.

a. Multiplicative group of integers modulo n
b. Discrete logarithm
c. Modular arithmetic
d. Chinese Remainder Theorem

12. A _____ is an n × n table filled with n different symbols in such a way that each symbol occurs exactly once in each row and exactly once in each column. Here is an example: $\begin{bmatrix} 1 & 2 & 3 \\ 2 & 3 & 1 \\ 3 & 1 & 2 \end{bmatrix}$

Latin squares occur as the multiplication tables of quasigroups. They have applications in the design of experiments and in error correcting codes.

a. Latin square
b. -module
c. -equivalence
d. 2-bridge knot

13. An _____ is a group satisfying the requirement that the result of applying the group operation to two group elements does not depend on their order Abelian groups generalize the arithmetic of addition of integers; they are named after Niels Henrik Abel.

The concept of an _____ is one of the first concepts encountered in undergraduate abstract algebra, with many other basic objects, such as a module and a vector space, being its refinements.

a. ADE classification
b. Elementary abelian group
c. Algebraically compact
d. Abelian group

14. In ring theory, a branch of abstract algebra, a _____ is a ring in which the multiplication operation is commutative. The study of commutative rings is called commutative algebra.

Some specific kinds of commutative rings are given with the following chain of class inclusions:

- commutative rings ⊃ integral domains ⊃ unique factorization domains ⊃ principal ideal domains ⊃ Euclidean domains ⊃ fields

A ring is a set R equipped with two binary operations, i.e. operations that combine any two elements of the ring to a third. They are called addition and multiplication and commonly denoted by '+' and '·', e.g. a + b and a · b.

a. Commutative ring
b. Nilradical
c. Differential calculus over commutative algebras
d. Going up

15. In mathematics, a _____ is a type of algebraic structure. There is some variation among mathematicians as to exactly what properties a _____ is required to have, as described in detail below. However, commonly a _____ is defined as a set together with two binary operations (usually called addition and multiplication), where each operation combines two elements to form a third element.

a. 2-bridge knot
b. -equivalence
c. -module
d. Ring

16. In mathematics, the _____, denoted by T (or in blackboard bold by $\mathbb{T}$), is the multiplicative group of all complex numbers with absolute value 1, i.e., the unit circle in the complex plane.

$$\mathbb{T} = \{z \in \mathbb{C} : |z| = 1\}.$$

The _____ forms a subgroup of $C^\times$, the multiplicative group of all nonzero complex numbers. Since $C^\times$ is abelian, it follows that T is as well.

a. Circle group
b. Power automorphism
c. Principal homogeneous space
d. Group object

17. In mathematics, the complex numbers are an extension of the real numbers obtained by adjoining an imaginary unit, denoted i, which satisfies:

$$i^2 = -1.$$

Every _____ can be written in the form a + bi, where a and b are real numbers called the real part and the imaginary part of the _____, respectively.

Complex numbers are a field, and thus have addition, subtraction, multiplication, and division operations. These operations extend the corresponding operations on real numbers, although with a number of additional elegant and useful properties, e.g., negative real numbers can be obtained by squaring complex (imaginary) numbers.

a. 2-bridge knot
b. -module
c. -equivalence
d. Complex number

18. In algebra, a _____ of an element in a quadratic extension field of a field K is its image under the unique non-identity automorphism of the extended field that fixes K. If the extension is generated by a square root of an element r of K, then the _____ of $a + b\sqrt{r}$ is $a - b\sqrt{r}$ for $a, b \in K$, and in particular in the case of the field C of complex numbers as an extension of the field R of real numbers (where r = − 1), the complex _____ of a + bi is a − bi.

Forming the sum or product of any element of the extension field with its _____ always gives an element of K. This can be used to rewrite a quotient of numbers in the extended field so that the denominator lies in K, by multiplying numerator and denominator by the _____ of the denominator. This process is called rationalization of the denominator, in particular if K is the field Q of rational numbers.

   a. Field arithmetic
   b. K-theory
   c. Digital root
   d. Conjugate

19. In mathematics, the _____ of two sets is the set of elements which are in one of the sets, but not in both. This operation is the set-theoretic kin of the exclusive disjunction (XOR operation) in Boolean logic. The _____ of the sets A and B is commonly denoted by

$$A \triangle B.$$

Venn diagram of A Δ B.
   a. Theory of equations
   b. Hecke algebra
   c. Symmetric difference
   d. Degree

20. A _____ is a complex number whose real and imaginary part are both integers. The Gaussian integers, with ordinary addition and multiplication of complex numbers, form an integral domain, usually written as Z[i]. This domain does not have a total ordering that respects arithmetic, since it contains imaginary numbers.
   a. Gaussian integer
   b. Jacobi sum
   c. Kummer sum
   d. Quadratic Gauss sums

Chapter 2. Groups I

21. In mathematics, the _____ of degree n is the set of n×n invertible matrices, together with the operation of ordinary matrix multiplication. This forms a group, because the product of two invertible matrices is again invertible, and the inverse of an invertible matrix is invertible. The name is because the columns of an invertible matrix are linearly independent, hence the vectors/points they define are in general linear position, and matrices in the _____ take points in general linear position to points in general linear position.

   a. Valuation ring
   b. Linearly independent
   c. Direct product
   d. General linear group

22. The _____ are natural numbers including 0 ' href='/wiki/0_(number)'>0, 1, 2, 3, ...) and their negatives (0, −1, −2, −3, ...). They are numbers that can be written without a fractional or decimal component, and fall within the set {...

   a. Integers
   b. ADE classification
   c. Abelian P-root group
   d. AKS primality test

23. In mathematics, a _____ is a rectangular array of numbers. This way, matrices can record data that depend on multiple parameters. In particular they are used to keep track of the coefficients of multiple linear equations. Matrices are closely connected to linear transformations, which are higher-dimensional analogs of linear functions, i.e., functions of the form f(x) = c · x, where c is a constant. This map corresponds to a _____ with one row and column, with entry c. In addition to a number of elementary, entrywise operations such as _____ addition a key notion is _____ multiplication, which displays a number of features not encountered in numbers; for example, products of matrices depend on the order of the factors, unlike products of real numbers, say, where c · d = d · c for any two numbers c and d.

   a. Commutativity
   b. Polynomial expression
   c. Heap
   d. Matrix

24. In mathematics, two vectors are _____ if they are perpendicular, i.e., they form a right angle. The word comes from the Greek ὀρθός, meaning 'straight', and γωνία (gonia), meaning 'angle'. For example, a subway and the street above, although they do not physically intersect, are _____ if they cross at a right angle.

   a. Unital
   b. Embedding
   c. Expression
   d. Orthogonal

25. In mathematics, the _____ or general _____ of any affine space over a field K is the group of all invertible affine transformations from the space into itself.

It is a Lie group if K is the real or complex field or quaternions.

Concretely, given a vector space V, it has an underlying affine space A obtained by e;forgettinge; the origin, with V acting by translations, and the _____ of A can be described concretely as the semidirect product of V by GL(V), the general linear group of V:

$$\mathrm{Aff}(A) = V \rtimes \mathrm{GL}(V)$$

The action of GL(V) on V is the natural one (linear transforms are automorphisms), so this defines a semidirect product.

   a. Affine group
   b. Affine transformation
   c. AKS primality test
   d. ADE classification

26. In mathematics, _____ is a property that a binary operation can have. It means that, within an expression containing two or more of the same associative operators in a row, the order that the operations are performed does not matter as long as the sequence of the operands is not changed. That is, rearranging the parentheses in such an expression will not change its value.

   a. Anticommutativity
   b. Associativity
   c. Identity element
   d. External

27. In group theory, a branch of mathematics, the term _____ is used in two closely related senses:

- the _____ of a group is its cardinality, i.e. the number of its elements;
- the _____, sometimes period, of an element a of a group is the smallest positive integer m such that $a^m = e$ (where e denotes the identity element of the group, and a^m denotes the product of m copies of a.) If no such m exists, we say that a has infinite _____. All elements of finite groups have finite _____.

We denote the _____ of a group G by ord(G) or $|G|$ and the _____ of an element a by ord(a) or $|a|$.

Example. The symmetric group S_3 has the following multiplication table.

This group has six elements, so ord(S_3) = 6.

   a. Index calculus algorithm
   b. Artin group
   c. Outer automorphism group
   d. Order

28. In linear algebra, a _____ is a linear transformation that squares to the identity ($R^2 = I$, where R is in K dimensional space), also known as an involution in the general linear group. In addition to reflections across hyperplanes, the class of general reflections includes point reflections, reflections across subspaces of intermediate dimension, and non-orthogonal reflections.

A _____ over a hyperplane in an inner product space is necessarily symmetric, but a general _____ need not be as the example $\begin{bmatrix} 1 & 0 \\ 1 & -1 \end{bmatrix}$ shows.

   a. Homomorphic secret sharing
   b. Shear mappings
   c. Morphism
   d. Reflection

29. In geometry and linear algebra, a _____ is a transformation in a plane or in space that describes the motion of a rigid body around a fixed point. A _____ is different from a translation, which has no fixed points, and from a reflection, which 'flips' the bodies it is transforming. A _____ and the above-mentioned transformations are isometries; they leave the distance between any two points unchanged after the transformation.

   a. Reflection
   b. Real matrices
   c. Shear mappings
   d. Rotation

30. In mathematics, a _____ is the group of symmetries of a regular polygon, including both rotations and reflections. Dihedral groups are among the simplest examples of finite groups, and they play an important role in group theory, geometry, and chemistry.

There are two competing notations for the _____ associated to a polygon with n sides.

a. Dihedral group
b. Group representations
c. Characteristic subgroup
d. Rank of a group

31. In mathematics, an _____ is the group of even permutations of a finite set. The _____ on the set {1,...,n} is called the _____ of degree n, or the _____ on n letters and denoted by A_n or Alt(n.)

For instance, the _____ of degree 4 is A_4 = {e, (123), (132), (124), (142), (134), (143), (234), (243), (12)(34), (13)(24), (14)(23)}

a. Alternating group
b. Octahedral symmetry
c. Extra special groups
d. Icosahedral symmetry

32. In group theory, a _____ is a group that can be generated by a single element, in the sense that the group has an element g (called a 'generator' of the group) such that, when written multiplicatively, every element of the group is a power of g (a multiple of g when the notation is additive.) The 6th complex roots of unity form a _____ under multiplication. ζ is a primitive element, but $ζ^2$ is not, because the odd powers of ζ are not a power of $ζ^2$.

A group G is called cyclic if there exists an element g in G such that G = <g> = { g^n | n is an integer }.

a. Torsion subgroup
b. Finitely generated abelian group
c. Locally cyclic group
d. Cyclic group

33. A _____ is a left or right _____ of some subgroup in G. Since Hg = g(g⁻¹Hg), the right cosets Hg (of H) and the left cosets g(g⁻¹Hg) (of the conjugate subgroup g⁻¹Hg) are the same. Hence it is not meaningful to speak of a _____ as being left or right unless one first specifies the underlying subgroup.

For abelian groups or groups written additively, the notation used changes to g+H and H+g respectively.

a. Coset
b. Burnside ring
c. Wreath product
d. Grigorchuk group

34. In mathematics, the _____ of degree n over a field F is the set of n×n matrices with determinant 1, with the group operations of ordinary matrix multiplication and matrix inversion. This is the normal subgroup of the general linear group, given by the kernel of the determinant

$$\det : \mathrm{GL}(n, F) \to F^\times.$$

where we write $F^\times$ for the multiplicative group of F (that is, excluding 0.)

These elements are 'special' in that they fall on a subvariety of the general linear group - they satisfy a polynomial equation (since the determinant is polynomial in the entries.)

a. Zero divisor
b. Simple
c. Semiring
d. Special linear group

35. A _____ between two algebras over a field K, A and B, is a map $F : A \to B$ such that for all k in K and x,y in A,

- F(kx) = kF(x)

- F(x + y) = F(x) + F(y)

- F(xy) = F(x)F(y)

If F is bijective then F is said to be an isomorphism between A and B.

Let A = K[x] be the set of all polynomials over a field K and B be the set of all polynomial functions over K. Both A and B are algebras over K given by the standard multiplication and addition of polynomials and functions, respectively. We can map each f in A to $\hat{f}$ in B by the rule $\hat{f}(t) = f(t)$. A routine check shows that the mapping $f \mapsto \hat{f}$ is a _____ of the algebras A and B. If K is a finite field then let

$$p(x) = \Pi_{t \in K}(x - t).$$

p is a nonzero polynomial in K[x], however $p(t) = 0$ for all t in K, so $\hat{p} = 0$ is the zero function and the algebras are not isomorphic.

a. Tensor algebra
b. Frobenius matrix
c. Tensor product of algebras
d. Homomorphism

36. In abstract algebra, an _____ is a bijective map f such that both f and its inverse f $^{-1}$ are homomorphisms, i.e., structure-preserving mappings. In the more general setting of category theory, an _____ is a morphism f:X→Y in a category for which there exists an 'inverse' f $^{-1}$:Y→X, with the property that both f $^{-1}$f=id$_X$ and ff $^{-1}$=id$_Y$.

Informally, an _____ is a kind of mapping between objects, which shows a relationship between two properties or operations.

a. Endomorphism
b. Isomorphism
c. Epimorphism
d. ADE classification

37. In mathematics, given two groups (G, *) and (H, Â·), a _____ from (G, *) to (H, Â·) is a function h : G → H such that for all u and v in G it holds that

$$h(u * v) = h(u) \cdot h(v)$$

where the group operation on the left hand side of the equation is that of G and on the right hand side that of H.

From this property, one can deduce that h maps the identity element e_G of G to the identity element e_H of H, and it also maps inverses to inverses in the sense that

$h(u^{-1}) = h(u)^{-1}$.

Hence one can say that h 'is compatible with the group structure'.

Older notations for the homomorphism h(x) may be x_h, though this may be confused as an index or a general subscript.

a. Metanilpotent group
b. Pair
c. Baby-step giant-step
d. Group homomorphism

38. In the various branches of mathematics that fall under the heading of abstract algebra, the _____ of a homomorphism measures the degree to which the homomorphism fails to be injective. An important special case is the _____ of a matrix, also called the null space.

The definition of _____ takes various forms in various contexts.

a. K-theory
b. Monomial basis
c. Completing the square
d. Kernel

39. In mathematics, more specifically in abstract algebra, a _____ is a special kind of subgroup. Normal subgroups are important because they can be used to construct quotient groups from a given group.

Évariste Galois was the first to realize the importance of the existence of normal subgroups.

a. Hanna Neumann conjecture
b. Characteristic subgroup
c. Cayley graph
d. Normal subgroup

40. The term _____ or centre is used in various contexts in abstract algebra to denote the set of all those elements that commute with all other elements. More specifically:

- The _____ of a group G consists of all those elements x in G such that xg = gx for all g in G. This is a normal subgroup of G.
- The _____ of a ring R is the subset of R consisting of all those elements x of R such that xr = rx for all r in R. The _____ is a commutative subring of R, so R is an algebra over its _____.
- The _____ of an algebra A consists of all those elements x of A such that xa = ax for all a in A. See also: central simple algebra.
- The _____ of a Lie algebra L consists of all those elements x in L such that [x,a] = 0 for all a in L. This is an ideal of the Lie algebra L.
- The _____ of a monoidal category C consists of pairs (A,u) where A is an object of C, and $u : A \otimes - \to - \otimes A$ a natural isomorphism satisfying certain axioms.

a. Self-adjoint
b. Left alternative
c. Ring theory
d. Center

41. _____, in mathematics, are a non-commutative number system that extends the complex numbers. The _____ were first described by Irish mathematician Sir William Rowan Hamilton in 1843 and applied to mechanics in three-dimensional space. They find uses in both theoretical and applied mathematics, in particular for calculations involving three-dimensional rotations , such as in 3D computer graphics, although they have been superseded in many applications by vectors and matrices.

a. Split-quaternions
b. Generalized quaternion interpolation
c. Split-biquaternion
d. Quaternions

42. In mathematics, specifically abstract algebra, the _____ are three theorems that describe the relationship between quotients, homomorphisms, and subobjects. Versions of the theorems exist for groups, rings, vector spaces, modules, Lie algebras, and various other algebraic structures. In universal algebra, the _____ can be generalized to the context of algebras and congruences.

a. AKS primality test
b. ADE classification
c. Identity theorem for Riemann surfaces
d. Isomorphism theorems

43. In mathematics, especially group theory, the elements of any group may be partitioned into conjugacy classes; members of the same _____ share many properties, and study of conjugacy classes of non-abelian groups reveals many important features of their structure. In all abelian groups every _____ is a set containing one element (singleton set.)

Functions that are constant for members of the same _____ are called class functions.

   a. Group isomorphism problem
   b. Maximal subgroup
   c. Homeomorphism group
   d. Conjugacy class

44. In algebra and geometry, a _____ is a way of describing symmetries of objects using groups. The essential elements of the object are described by a set and the symmetries of the object are described by the symmetry group of this set, which consists of bijective transformations of the set. In this case, the group is also called a permutation group (especially if the set is finite or not a vector space) or transformation group (especially if the set is a vector space and the group acts like linear transformations of the set.)
   a. Group action
   b. Group
   c. Free group
   d. Modular group

45. In group theory, the _____ and normalizer of a subset S of a group G are subgroups of G which have a restricted action on the elements of S and S as a whole, respectively. These subgroups provide insight into the structure of G.

The _____ of an element a of a group G (written as $C_G(a)$) is the set of elements of G which commute with a; in other words, $C_G(a) = \{x \in G : xa = ax\}$.

   a. HN group
   b. Class automorphism
   c. Stallings' theorem about ends of groups
   d. Centralizer

46. The iterated wreath products of cyclic groups of order p are very important examples of _____. Denote the cyclic group of order p as W(1), and the wreath product of W(n) with W(1) as W(n+1.) Then W(n) is the Sylow p-subgroup of the symmetric group $Sym(p^n)$.

a. History of group theory
b. Group representations
c. Polycyclic group
d. P-groups

47. In mathematics, the term _____ is used to describe an algebraic structures which in some sense cannot be divided by a smaller structure of the same type. Put another way, an algebraic structure is _____ if the kernel of every homomorphism is either the whole structure or a single element. Some examples are:

- A group is called a _____ group if it does not contain a non-trivial proper normal subgroup.
- A ring is called a _____ ring if it does not contain a non-trivial two sided ideal.
- A module is called a _____ module if does not contain a non-trivial submodule.
- An algebra is called a _____ algebra if does not contain a non-trivial two sided ideal.

The general pattern is that the structure admits no non-trivial congruence relations.

a. Linear combinations
b. Simple
c. Commutativity
d. Polarization identity

48. In mathematics, specifically group theory, the _____ of a subgroup H in a group G is the e;relative sizee; of H in G. For example, if H has _____ 2 in G, then intuitively e;halfe; of the elements of G lie in H. The _____ of H in G is usually denoted $|G : H|$ or [G : H].

If G and H are finite groups, then the _____ of H in G is simply the quotient of the orders of the two groups:

$$|G : H| = \frac{|G|}{|H|}.$$

By Lagrange's theorem, this number is always a positive integer.

If G and H are infinite, then the _____ of H is G is defined as the number of cosets of H in G.

a. Inner automorphism
b. Outer automorphism
c. Index
d. Even permutations

Chapter 3. Commutative Rings I

1. In mathematics, and in particular in abstract algebra, distributivity is a property of binary operations that generalises the _____ from elementary algebra. For example: <_____>
    2 × (1 + 3) = (2 × 1) + (2 × 3.)

In the left-hand side of the above equation, the 2 multiplies the sum of 1 and 3; on the right-hand side, it multiplies the 1 and the 3 individually, with the results added afterwards.

   a. 2-bridge knot
   b. Distributive law
   c. -equivalence
   d. -module

2. The _____ is a result about congruences in number theory and its generalizations in abstract algebra.

The original form of the theorem, contained in a third-century AD book Sun Zi suanjing by Chinese mathematician Sun Tzu and later republished in a 1247 book by Qin Jiushao, the Shushu Jiuzhang (æ•¸æ›¸ä¹ ç« Mathematical Treatise in Nine Sections) is a statement about simultaneous congruences

Suppose n_1, n_2, â€¦, n_k are positive integers which are pairwise coprime.

   a. Modular arithmetic
   b. Multiplicative group of integers modulo n
   c. Chinese Remainder Theorem
   d. Discrete logarithm

3. A _____ is an n × n table filled with n different symbols in such a way that each symbol occurs exactly once in each row and exactly once in each column. Here is an example: $\begin{bmatrix} 1 & 2 & 3 \\ 2 & 3 & 1 \\ 3 & 1 & 2 \end{bmatrix}$

Latin squares occur as the multiplication tables of quasigroups. They have applications in the design of experiments and in error correcting codes.

   a. -equivalence
   b. Latin square
   c. -module
   d. 2-bridge knot

Chapter 3. Commutative Rings I

4. In ring theory, a branch of abstract algebra, a _____ is a ring in which the multiplication operation is commutative. The study of commutative rings is called commutative algebra.

Some specific kinds of commutative rings are given with the following chain of class inclusions:

- commutative rings ⊃ integral domains ⊃ unique factorization domains ⊃ principal ideal domains ⊃ Euclidean domains ⊃ fields

A ring is a set R equipped with two binary operations, i.e. operations that combine any two elements of the ring to a third. They are called addition and multiplication and commonly denoted by '+' and '·', e.g. a + b and a · b.

   a. Commutative ring
   b. Differential calculus over commutative algebras
   c. Nilradical
   d. Going up

5. In mathematics, a _____ is a type of algebraic structure. There is some variation among mathematicians as to exactly what properties a _____ is required to have, as described in detail below. However, commonly a _____ is defined as a set together with two binary operations (usually called addition and multiplication), where each operation combines two elements to form a third element.
   a. -equivalence
   b. Ring
   c. 2-bridge knot
   d. -module

6. A _____ is a complex number whose real and imaginary part are both integers. The Gaussian integers, with ordinary addition and multiplication of complex numbers, form an integral domain, usually written as Z[i]. This domain does not have a total ordering that respects arithmetic, since it contains imaginary numbers.
   a. Jacobi sum
   b. Quadratic Gauss sums
   c. Kummer sum
   d. Gaussian integer

7. The _____ are natural numbers including 0 ' href='/wiki/0_(number)'>0, 1, 2, 3, ...) and their negatives (0, −1, −2, −3, ...). They are numbers that can be written without a fractional or decimal component, and fall within the set {...

Chapter 3. Commutative Rings I

a. AKS primality test
b. Integers
c. ADE classification
d. Abelian P-root group

8. In mathematics, especially in the area of abstract algebra known as ring theory, a _____ is a ring with $0 \neq 1$ such that ab = 0 implies that either a = 0 or b = 0 (the zero-product property.) That is, it is a nontrivial ring without left or right zero divisors. A commutative _____ is called an integral _____.
    a. Coherent ring
    b. Partially-ordered ring
    c. Subring
    d. Domain

9. _____ is one of the four basic arithmetic operations; it is the inverse of addition, meaning that if we start with any number and add any number and then subtract the same number we added, we return to the number we started with. _____ is denoted by a minus sign in infix notation.

The traditional names for the parts of the formula

$$c - b = a$$

are minuend (c) − subtrahend (b) = difference (a.)

a. -module
b. -equivalence
c. 2-bridge knot
d. Subtraction

10. In mathematics, a _____ is a subset of a ring, which contains the multiplicative identity and is itself a ring under the same binary operations. Naturally, those authors who do not require rings to contain a multiplicative identity do not require subrings to possess the identity (if it exists.) This leads to the added advantage that ideals become subrings
    a. Kurosh problem
    b. Poisson ring
    c. Semiperfect ring
    d. Subring

11. In algebraic geometry, divisors are a generalization of codimension one subvarieties of algebraic varieties; two different generalizations are in common use, Cartier divisors and Weil divisors The concepts agree on non-singular varieties over algebraically closed fields.

A Weil _____ is a locally finite linear combination (with integral coefficients) of irreducible subvarieties of codimension one.

   a. Picard group
   b. Linear system of divisors
   c. Lefschetz pencil
   d. Divisor

12. In mathematics, _____ are a concept central to linear algebra and related fields of mathematics

Suppose that K is a field and V is a vector space over K. As usual, we call elements of V vectors and call elements of K scalars.

   a. Groupoid
   b. Hyperstructures
   c. Left alternative
   d. Linear combinations

13. In mathematics, a _____ in a (unital) ring R is an invertible element of R, i.e. an element u such that there is a v in R with

$$uv = vu = 1_R$$, where 1_R is the multiplicative identity element.

That is, u is an invertible element of the multiplicative monoid of R. If $0 \neq 1$ in the ring, then 0 is not a _____.

Unfortunately, the term _____ is also used to refer to the identity element 1_R of the ring, in expressions like ring with a _____ or _____ ring, and also e.g. '_____' matrix.

   a. Ore condition
   b. Unit
   c. Ore extension
   d. Ascending chain condition on principal ideals

Chapter 3. Commutative Rings I

14. In mathematics, a _____ is a group associated with a certain type of field extension. The study of field extensions (and polynomials which give rise to them) via Galois groups is called Galois theory after Évariste Galois who first invented them
   a. Field of fractions
   b. Splitting field
   c. Galois group
   d. Primitive element theorem

15. In elementary algebra, a _____ is a polynomial with two terms--the sum of two monomials--often bound by parenthesis or brackets when operated upon. It is the simplest kind of polynomial other than monomials.

   - The _____ $a^2 - b^2$ can be factored as the product of two other binomials:

     $a^2 - b^2 = (a + b)(a - b.)$

     This is a special case of the more general formula:

     $$a^{n+1} - b^{n+1} = (a - b) \sum_{k=0}^{n} a^k b^{n-k}$$

   - The product of a pair of linear binomials (ax + b) and (cx + d) is:

     $(ax + b)(cx + d) = acx^2 + axd + bcx + bd.$

   - A _____ raised to the nth power, represented as

     $(a + b)^n$

     can be expanded by means of the _____ theorem or, equivalently, using Pascal's triangle. Taking a simple example, the perfect square _____ $(p + q)^2$ can be found by squaring the first digit, adding twice the product of the first and second digit and finally adding the square of the second digit, to give $p^2 + 2pq + q^2$.

   a. Content
   b. Theory of equations
   c. Generalized arithmetic progression
   d. Binomial

16. In mathematics, the _____ is an important formula giving the expansion of powers of sums. Its simplest version states that

$$(x + y)^n = \sum_{k=0}^{n} \binom{n}{k} x^{n-k} y^k \qquad (1)$$

for any real or complex numbers x and y, and any non-negative integer n. The binomial coefficient appearing in (1) may be defined in terms of the factorial function n!:

$$\binom{n}{k} = \frac{n!}{k!\,(n-k)!}.$$

For example, here are the cases where 2 ≤ n ≤ 5:

$$(x+y)^2 = x^2 + 2xy + y^2$$
$$(x+y)^3 = x^3 + 3x^2y + 3xy^2 + y^3$$
$$(x+y)^4 = x^4 + 4x^3y + 6x^2y^2 + 4xy^3 + y^4$$
$$(x+y)^5 = x^5 + 5x^4y + 10x^3y^2 + 10x^2y^3 + 5xy^4 + y^5.$$

Formula (1) is valid more generally for any elements x and y of a semiring as long as xy = yx.

a. -module
b. 2-bridge knot
c. -equivalence
d. Binomial theorem

17. A _____ is a set G closed under a binary operation · satisfying the following 3 axioms:

- Associativity: For all a, b and c in G, (a · b) · c = a · (b · c.)
- Identity element: There exists an e∈G such that for all a in G, e · a = a · e = a.
- Inverse element: For each a in G, there is an element b in G such that a · b = b · a = e, where e is an identity element.

Basic examples for groups are the integers Z with addition operation, or rational numbers without zero Q{0} with multiplication. More generally, for any ring R, the units in R form a multiplicative _____ Groups include, however, much more general structures than the above.

a. Grigorchuk group
b. Product of group subsets
c. Nilpotent group
d. Group

18. In mathematics, a _____ R is a ring (with identity) for which $x^2 = x$ for all x in R; that is, R consists only of idempotent elements.

Chapter 3. Commutative Rings I

Boolean rings are automatically commutative and of characteristic 2 A _____ is essentially the same thing as a Boolean algebra, with ring multiplication corresponding to conjunction or meet ∧, and ring addition to exclusive disjunction or symmetric difference (not disjunction ∨.)

  a. Hereditary
  b. Domain
  c. Ring of integers
  d. Boolean ring

19. In abstract algebra, a _____ is an algebraic structure with notions of addition, subtraction, multiplication and division, satisfying certain axioms. The most commonly used fields are the _____ of real numbers, the _____ of complex numbers, and the _____ of rational numbers, but there are also finite fields, fields of functions, various algebraic number fields, p-adic fields, and so forth.

Any _____ may be used as the scalars for a vector space, which is the standard general context for linear algebra.

  a. Tensor product of fields
  b. Separable
  c. Generic polynomial
  d. Field

20. In its simplest meaning in mathematics and logic, an _____ is an action or procedure which produces a new value from one or more input values. There are two common types of operations: unary and binary. Unary operations involve only one value, such as negation and trigonometric functions.
  a. Operation
  b. AKS primality test
  c. ADE classification
  d. Abelian P-root group

21. In mathematics, a _____ is a constant multiplicative factor of a certain object. For example, in the expression $9x^2$, the _____ of x^2 is 9.

The object can be such things as a variable, a vector, a function, etc.

a. Tschirnhaus transformation
b. Coefficient
c. Constant term
d. Vandermonde polynomial

22. In mathematics, there are several meanings of _____ depending on the subject.

A _____, usually denoted by ° (the _____ symbol), is a measurement of plane angle, representing $1/360$ of a full rotation. When that angle is with respect to a reference meridian, it indicates a location along a great circle of a sphere, such as Earth , Mars, or the celestial sphere.

a. Relation algebra
b. Symmetric difference
c. Median algebra
d. Degree

23. A _____ is a symbol that stands for a value that may vary; the term usually occurs in opposition to constant, which is a symbol for a non-varying value, i.e. completely fixed or fixed in the context of use. The concepts of constants and variables are fundamental to all modern mathematics, science, engineering, and computer programming.

Much of the basic theory for which we use variables today, such as school geometry and algebra, was developed thousands of years ago, but the use of symbolic formulae and variables is only several hundreds of years old.

a. 2-bridge knot
b. Variable
c. -module
d. -equivalence

24. In mathematics, the _____ of a polynomial is the term of degree 0. For example, in the polynomial

$$X^3 + 2X + 3$$

over the variable X, the _____ is 3. Here, the _____ is given by a numeral, but it may also be specified by a letter that is a parameter rather than a variable, as in the polynomial

$$ax^2 + bx + c,$$

in the variable x, where a, b, and c are parameters so that c is the _____.

a. Constant term
b. Characteristic polynomial
c. Symmetric polynomial
d. Quadratic function

25. _____ or biquadratic reciprocity is a collection of theorems in elementary and algebraic number theory that state conditions under which the congruence $x^4 \equiv p \pmod{q}$ is solvable; the word 'reciprocity' comes from the form of some of these theorems, in that they relate the solvability of the congruence $x^4 \equiv p \pmod{q}$ to that of $x^4 \equiv q \pmod{p}$.

Euler made the first conjectures about biquadratic reciprocity. Gauss published two monographs on biquadratic reciprocity.

a. Quartic
b. Cyclotomic character
c. Modulus
d. Herbrand quotient

26. In mathematics, a _____ is any function which can be written as the ratio of two polynomial functions. _____ of degree 2: $y = \dfrac{x^2 - 3x - 2}{x^2 - 4}$

In the case of one variable, x, a _____ is a function of the form

$$f(x) = \frac{P(x)}{Q(x)}$$

where P and Q are polynomial function in x and Q is not the zero polynomial. The domain of f is the set of all points x for which the denominator Q(x) is not zero.

a. -equivalence
b. -module
c. Legendre rational functions
d. Rational function

27. The _____ is often met for the first time as an operation on a single real function of a single real variable. One of the simplest settings for generalizations is to vector valued functions of several variables (most often the domain forms a vector space as well.) This is the field of multivariable calculus.

a. -module
b. -equivalence
c. 2-bridge knot
d. Derivative

28. In mathematics, _____ are devices that make it possible to employ much of the analytical machinery of power series in settings that do not have natural notions of convergence. They are also useful, especially in combinatorics, for providing compact representations of sequences and multisets, and for finding closed formulas for recursively defined sequences; this is known as the method of generating functions.

A _____ can be loosely thought of as a polynomial with infinitely many terms.

a. Multiplicative group
b. Formal power series
c. Cokernel
d. Matrix

29. A _____ between two algebras over a field K, A and B, is a map $F : A \to B$ such that for all k in K and x,y in A,

- $F(kx) = kF(x)$

- $F(x + y) = F(x) + F(y)$

- $F(xy) = F(x)F(y)$

If F is bijective then F is said to be an isomorphism between A and B.

Let A = K[x] be the set of all polynomials over a field K and B be the set of all polynomial functions over K. Both A and B are algebras over K given by the standard multiplication and addition of polynomials and functions, respectively. We can map each f in A to $\hat{f}$ in B by the rule $\hat{f}(t) = f(t)$. A routine check shows that the mapping $f \mapsto \hat{f}$ is a _____ of the algebras A and B. If K is a finite field then let

$$p(x) = \Pi_{t \in K}(x - t).$$

p is a nonzero polynomial in K[x], however $p(t) = 0$ for all t in K, so $\hat{p} = 0$ is the zero function and the algebras are not isomorphic.

Chapter 3. Commutative Rings I

a. Tensor product of algebras
b. Tensor algebra
c. Frobenius matrix
d. Homomorphism

30. In abstract algebra, an _____ is a bijective map f such that both f and its inverse f^{-1} are homomorphisms, i.e., structure-preserving mappings. In the more general setting of category theory, an _____ is a morphism f:X→Y in a category for which there exists an 'inverse' f^{-1}:Y→X, with the property that both $f^{-1}f=id_X$ and $ff^{-1}=id_Y$.

Informally, an _____ is a kind of mapping between objects, which shows a relationship between two properties or operations.

a. Epimorphism
b. Isomorphism
c. ADE classification
d. Endomorphism

31. In ring theory, a branch of abstract algebra, an _____ is a special subset of a ring. The _____ concept generalizes in an appropriate way some important properties of integers like 'even number' or 'multiple of 3'.

For instance, in rings one studies prime ideals instead of prime numbers, one defines coprime ideals as a generalization of coprime numbers, and one can prove a generalized Chinese remainder theorem about ideals.

a. Ideal
b. AKS primality test
c. Augmentation ideal
d. ADE classification

32. In ring theory or abstract algebra, a _____ is a function between two rings which respects the operations of addition and multiplication.

More precisely, if R and S are rings, then a _____ is a function f : R → S such that

- f(a + b) = f(a) + f(b) for all a and b in R
- f(ab) = f(a) f(b) for all a and b in R
- f(1) = 1

Naturally, if one does not require rings to have a multiplicative identity then the last condition is dropped.

The composition of two ring homomorphisms is a _____. It follows that the class of all rings forms a category with ring homomorphisms as the morphisms (cf.

a. Krull ring
b. Group ring
c. Global dimension
d. Ring homomorphism

33. In ring theory, a branch of abstract algebra, a _____ is an ideal I in a ring R that is generated by a single element a of R.

More specifically:

- a left _____ of R is a subset of R of the form Ra := {ra : r in R};
- a right _____ is a subset of the form aR := {ar : r in R};
- a two-sided _____ is a subset of the form RaR := {$r_1 a s_1$ + ... + $r_n a s_n$: $r_1, s_1,...,r_n, s_n$ in R}.

If R is a commutative ring, then the above three notions are all the same. In that case, it is common to write the ideal generated by a as (a.)

Not all ideals are principal.

a. Radical of an ring
b. Primitive ideal
c. Radical of an ideal
d. Principal ideal

34. In mathematics, one can often define a _____ of objects already known, giving a new one. This is generally the Cartesian product of the underlying sets, together with a suitably defined structure on the product set. More abstractly, one talks about the product in category theory, which formalizes these notions.

a. Group extension
b. Precedence rule
c. Special linear group
d. Direct product

35. In mathematics, a _____ of a number x is any number which, when repeatedly multiplied by itself, eventually yields x:

Chapter 3. Commutative Rings I

$$r \times r \times \cdots \times r = x.$$

In terms of exponentiation, r is a _____ of x if

$$r^n = x$$

for some positive integer n. For example, 2 is a _____ of 16 since $2^4 = 2 \times 2 \times 2 \times 2 = 16$.

The number n is called the degree of the _____.

a. Difference of two squares
b. Cubic function
c. Rationalisation
d. Root

36. In linear algebra, a _____ is a set of vectors that, in a linear combination, can represent every vector in a given vector space or free module, and such that no element of the set can be represented as a linear combination of the others. In other words, a _____ is a linearly independent spanning set.
a. Minor
b. Basis
c. Chirality
d. Supergroup

37. In abstract algebra, a _____ i.e., can be generated by a single element. More generally, a principal ring is a nonzero commutative ring whose ideals are principal, although some authors (e.g., Bourbaki) refers to Principal ideal domains as principal rings. The distinction being that a principal ideal ring may have zero divisors whereas a _____ cannot.
a. Minimal prime
b. Discrete valuation
c. Nilradical
d. Principal ideal domain

38. In mathematics, the adjective _____ means that an object cannot be expressed as a product of more than one non-trivial factors in a given set. See also factorization.

For any field F, the ring of polynomials with coefficients in F is denoted by F[x].

a. Alternating polynomial
b. Irreducible
c. Integer-valued polynomial
d. Ehrhart polynomial

39. In linear algebra, functional analysis and related areas of mathematics, a _____ is a function that assigns a strictly positive length or size to all vectors in a vector space, other than the zero vector. A seminorm (or pseudonorm), on the other hand, is allowed to assign zero length to some non-zero vectors.

A simple example is the 2-dimensional Euclidean space R^2 equipped with the Euclidean _____.

a. -module
b. Quasinorm
c. Norm
d. -equivalence

40. In mathematics, _____ or factoring is the decomposition of an object ' href='/wiki/Matrix_(mathematics)'>matrix) into a product of other objects, or factors, which when multiplied together give the original. For example, the number 15 factors into primes as 3 × 5, and the polynomial $x^2 - 4$ factors as $(x - 2)(x + 2)$. In all cases, a product of simpler objects is obtained.
a. 2-bridge knot
b. -equivalence
c. -module
d. Factorization

41. This article deals with the ring of complex numbers integral over Z. For the general notion of _____, see Integrality.

In number theory, an _____ is a complex number that is a root of some monic polynomial (leading coefficient 1) with coefficients in Z. The set of all algebraic integers is closed under addition and multiplication and therefore is a subring of complex numbers denoted by A. The ring A is the integral closure of regular integers Z in complex numbers.

The ring of integers of a number field K, denoted by O_K, is the intersection of K and A: it can also be characterised as the maximal order of the field K. Each _____ belongs to the ring of integers of some number field.

Chapter 3. Commutative Rings I

a. Algebraic number theory
b. Adele ring
c. Additive polynomial
d. Algebraic integer

42. In field theory, a branch of mathematics, a _____ is the minimal polynomial of a primitive element of the finite extension field GF(p^m.) In other words, a polynomial F(X) with coefficients in GF(p) = Z/pZ is a _____ if it has a root α in GF(p^m) such that $\{0, 1, \alpha, \alpha^2, \alpha^3, \ldots, \alpha^{p^m-2}\}$ is the entire field GF(p^m), and moreover, F(X) is the smallest degree polynomial having α as root.

In ring theory, the term _____ is used for a different purpose, to mean a polynomial over a unique factorization domain (such as the integers) whose greatest common divisor of its coefficients is a unit.

a. Formally real field
b. Kummer theory
c. Separable
d. Primitive polynomial

43. In algebra, the _____ of a polynomial is the highest common factor of its coefficients.

A polynomial is primitive if it has _____ unity.

Gauss's lemma for polynomials may be expressed as stating that for polynomials over a unique factorization domain, the _____ of the product of two polynomials is the product of their contents.

a. Nested radical
b. Filtration
c. Permanent
d. Content

44. In algebra, a _____ of an element in a quadratic extension field of a field K is its image under the unique non-identity automorphism of the extended field that fixes K. If the extension is generated by a square root of an element r of K, then the _____ of $a + b\sqrt{r}$ is $a - b\sqrt{r}$ for $a, b \in K$, and in particular in the case of the field C of complex numbers as an extension of the field R of real numbers (where r = − 1), the complex _____ of a + bi is a − bi.

Forming the sum or product of any element of the extension field with its _____ always gives an element of K. This can be used to rewrite a quotient of numbers in the extended field so that the denominator lies in K, by multiplying numerator and denominator by the _____ of the denominator. This process is called rationalization of the denominator, in particular if K is the field Q of rational numbers.

a. K-theory
b. Field arithmetic
c. Digital root
d. Conjugate

45. In a totally ordered set all elements are mutually comparable, so such a set can have at most one minimal element and at most one maximal element. Then, due to mutual comparability, the minimal element will also be the least element and the maximal element will also be the greatest element. Thus in a totally ordered set we can simply use the terms _____ and maximum.
   a. 2-bridge knot
   b. -module
   c. Minimum
   d. -equivalence

46. In algebra, the nth _____, for any positive integer n, is the monic polynomial

where the product is over all primitive n^{th} roots of unity ω, i.e. all the complex numbers ω of order n.

The degree of Φ_n, or in other words the number of factors in its definition above, is φ(n), where φ is Euler's totient function.

The coefficients of Φ_n are integers.

   a. Q-Vandermonde identity
   b. Character group
   c. Cyclic number
   d. Cyclotomic polynomial

47. In mathematics a _____ is a construction in ring theory, quite similar to the factor groups of group theory and the quotient spaces of linear algebra. One starts with a ring R and a two-sided ideal I in R, and constructs a new ring, the _____ R/I, essentially by requiring that all elements of I be zero. Intuitively, the _____ R/I is a 'simplified version' of R where the elements of I are 'ignored'.
   a. Quotient ring
   b. Domain
   c. Monoid ring
   d. Subring

48. In mathematics, specifically abstract algebra, the _____ are three theorems that describe the relationship between quotients, homomorphisms, and subobjects. Versions of the theorems exist for groups, rings, vector spaces, modules, Lie algebras, and various other algebraic structures. In universal algebra, the _____ can be generalized to the context of algebras and congruences.

   a. Isomorphism theorems
   b. AKS primality test
   c. ADE classification
   d. Identity theorem for Riemann surfaces

49. In mathematics, the _____ of a ring R, often denoted char(R), is defined to be the smallest number of times one must add the ring's multiplicative identity element (1) to itself to get the additive identity element (0); the ring is said to have _____ zero if this repeated sum never reaches the additive identity. That is, char(R) is the smallest positive number n such that

$$\underbrace{1 + \cdots + 1}_{n \text{ summands}} = 0$$

if such a number n exists, and 0 otherwise. The _____ may also be taken to be the exponent of the ring's additive group, that is, the smallest positive n such that

$$\underbrace{a + \cdots + a}_{n \text{ summands}} = 0$$

for every element a of the ring (again, if n exists; otherwise zero.)

   a. Characteristic
   b. Coherent ring
   c. Free ideal ring
   d. Hereditary

50. In mathematics, a field F is said to be _____ if every polynomial in one variable of degree at least 1, with coefficients in F, has a root in F.

As an example, the field of real numbers is not _____, because the polynomial equation $x^2 + 1 = 0$ has no solution in real numbers, even though all its coefficients (1 and 0) are real. The same argument proves that no subfield of the real field is _____; in particular, the field of rational numbers is not _____.

a. Ordered exponential
b. Unique factorization domain
c. Algebraically closed
d. Inverse semigroup

51. In mathematics, the _____, denoted by ⊗, is an operation on two matrices of arbitrary size resulting in a block matrix. It is a special case of a tensor product. The _____ should not be confused with the usual matrix multiplication, which is an entirely different operation.
   a. Laplace expansion
   b. Kronecker product
   c. Totally positive matrix
   d. Schur decomposition

52. In mathematics, two vectors are _____ if they are perpendicular, i.e., they form a right angle. The word comes from the Greek ἀρθός , meaning 'straight', and γωνία (gonia), meaning 'angle'. For example, a subway and the street above, although they do not physically intersect, are _____ if they cross at a right angle.
   a. Expression
   b. Unital
   c. Embedding
   d. Orthogonal

53. In mathematics, a _____ is a flat surface. Planes can arise as subspaces of some higher dimensional space, as with the walls of a room, or they may enjoy an independent existence in their own right, as in the setting of Euclidean geometry
   a. -equivalence
   b. Similarity
   c. -module
   d. Plane

54. In group theory, a branch of mathematics, the term _____ is used in two closely related senses:

   - the _____ of a group is its cardinality, i.e. the number of its elements;
   - the _____, sometimes period, of an element a of a group is the smallest positive integer m such that $a^m = e$ (where e denotes the identity element of the group, and a^m denotes the product of m copies of a.) If no such m exists, we say that a has infinite _____. All elements of finite groups have finite _____.

We denote the _____ of a group G by ord(G) or $|G|$ and the _____ of an element a by ord(a) or $|a|$.

Example. The symmetric group S_3 has the following multiplication table.

This group has six elements, so ord(S_3) = 6.

a. Artin group
b. Index calculus algorithm
c. Outer automorphism group
d. Order

Chapter 4. Goodies

1. In geometry, a _____ is a quadrilateral with two sets of parallel sides. The opposite or facing sides of a _____ are of equal length, and the opposite angles of a _____ are of equal size. The three-dimensional counterpart of a _____ is a parallelepiped.
    a. -equivalence
    b. 2-bridge knot
    c. Parallelogram
    d. -module

2. The real component of a quaternion is also called its _____ part.

    The term is also sometimes used informally to mean a vector, matrix, tensor, or other usually 'compound' value that is actually reduced to a single component. Thus, for example, the product of a 1×n matrix and an n×1 matrix, which is formally a 1×1 matrix, is often said to be a _____.

    a. Tensor product
    b. Self-adjoint
    c. Distributivity
    d. Scalar

3. In linear algebra, a family of vectors is _____ if none of them can be written as a linear combination of finitely many other vectors in the collection. A family of vectors which is not _____ is called linearly dependent. For instance, in the three-dimensional real vector space $\mathbb{R}^3$ we have the following example.
    a. Composition ring
    b. Derivative algebra
    c. Linearly independent
    d. Grothendieck group

4. In linear algebra, a _____ is a set of vectors that, in a linear combination, can represent every vector in a given vector space or free module, and such that no element of the set can be represented as a linear combination of the others. In other words, a _____ is a linearly independent spanning set.
    a. Basis
    b. Minor
    c. Chirality
    d. Supergroup

5. In mathematics, the _____ for a Euclidean space consists of one unit vector pointing in the direction of each axis of the Cartesian coordinate system. For example, the _____ for the Euclidean plane are the vectors

$$\mathbf{e}_x = (1,0), \quad \mathbf{e}_y = (0,1),$$

and the _____ for three-dimensional space are the vectors

$$\mathbf{e}_x = (1,0,0), \quad \mathbf{e}_y = (0,1,0), \quad \mathbf{e}_z = (0,0,1).$$

Here the vector e_x points in the x direction, the vector e_y points in the y direction, and the vector e_z points in the z direction. There are several common notations for these vectors, including $\{e_x, e_y, e_z\}$, $\{e_1, e_2, e_3\}$, $\{i, j, k\}$, and $\{x, y, z\}$.

a. 2-bridge knot
b. -equivalence
c. -module
d. Standard basis

6. In mathematics, the _____ of a vector space V is the cardinality (i.e. the number of vectors) of a basis of V. It is sometimes called Hamel _____ or algebraic _____ to distinguish it from other types of _____. All bases of a vector space have equal cardinality and so the _____ of a vector space is uniquely defined. The _____ of the vector space V over the field F can be written as $\dim_F(V)$ or as [V : F], read '_____ of V over F'.

a. Dual basis
b. Partial trace
c. Dimension
d. Cofactor

7. A _____ is an n × n table filled with n different symbols in such a way that each symbol occurs exactly once in each row and exactly once in each column. Here is an example: $\begin{bmatrix} 1 & 2 & 3 \\ 2 & 3 & 1 \\ 3 & 1 & 2 \end{bmatrix}$

Latin squares occur as the multiplication tables of quasigroups. They have applications in the design of experiments and in error correcting codes.

a. Latin square
b. -module
c. 2-bridge knot
d. -equivalence

8. In mathematics, two vectors are _____ if they are perpendicular, i.e., they form a right angle. The word comes from the Greek á½€ρθïŒς , meaning 'straight', and γωνῑα (gonia), meaning 'angle'. For example, a subway and the street above, although they do not physically intersect, are _____ if they cross at a right angle.

   a. Orthogonal
   b. Embedding
   c. Expression
   d. Unital

9. In discrete mathematics and predominantly in set theory, a _____ is a concept used in comparisons of sets to refer to the unique values of one set in relation to another. The terms 'absolute' and 'relative' _____ refer to more specific applications of the concept, with universal complements referring to elements unique to the universal set and the latter referring to the unique elements of one set in relation to another. In this image, the universal set is represented by the border of the image, and the set A as a disc.

   a. -module
   b. -equivalence
   c. Complement
   d. Pointed set

10. In the mathematical fields of linear algebra and functional analysis, the _____ $W^\perp$ of a subspace W of an inner product space V is the set of all vectors in V that are orthogonal to every vector in W, i.e., it is

$$W^\perp = \{x \in V : \langle x, y \rangle = 0 \text{ for all } y \in W\}.$$

Informally, it is called the perp, short for perpendicular complement.

The _____ is always closed in the metric topology. In finite-dimensional spaces, that is merely an instance of the fact that all subspaces of a vector space are closed.

   a. Invariant subspace
   b. Orthogonal complement
   c. Euclidean subspace
   d. Independent equation

11. In mathematics, a _____ is a rectangular array of numbers. This way, matrices can record data that depend on multiple parameters. In particular they are used to keep track of the coefficients of multiple linear equations. Matrices are closely connected to linear transformations, which are higher-dimensional analogs of linear functions, i.e., functions of the form f(x) = c · x, where c is a constant. This map corresponds to a _____ with one row and column, with entry c. In addition to a number of elementary, entrywise operations such as _____ addition a key notion is _____ multiplication, which displays a number of features not encountered in numbers; for example, products of matrices depend on the order of the factors, unlike products of real numbers, say, where c · d = d · c for any two numbers c and d.
   a. Polynomial expression
   b. Matrix
   c. Heap
   d. Commutativity

12. If $A_1, A_2, ..., A_n$ are _____ square matrices over a field, then

$$(A_1 A_2 \cdots A_n)^{-1} = A_n^{-1} A_{n-1}^{-1} \cdots A_1^{-1}.$$

It becomes evident why this is the case if one attempts to find an inverse for the product of the A_is from first principles, that is, that we wish to determine B such that

$$(A_1 A_2 \cdots A_n) B = I$$

where B is the inverse matrix of the product. To remove A_1 from the product, we can then write

$$A_1^{-1}(A_1 A_2 \cdots A_n) B = A_1^{-1} I$$

which would reduce the equation to

$$(A_2 A_3 \cdots A_n) B = A_1^{-1} I.$$

Likewise, then, from

$$A_2^{-1}(A_2 A_3 \cdots A_n) B = A_2^{-1} A_1^{-1} I$$

which simplifies to

$$(A_3 A_4 \cdots A_n) B = A_2^{-1} A_1^{-1} I.$$

If one repeat the process up to A_n, the equation becomes

$$B = A_n^{-1} A_{n-1}^{-1} \cdots A_2^{-1} A_1^{-1} I$$

$$B = A_n^{-1} A_{n-1}^{-1} \cdots A_2^{-1} A_1^{-1}$$

but B is the inverse matrix, i.e. $B = (A_1 A_2 \cdots A_n)^{-1}$ so the property is established.

Over the field of real numbers, the set of singular n-by-n matrices, considered as a subset of $R^{n \times n}$, is a null set, i.e., has Lebesgue measure zero.

a. -equivalence
b. Nonsingular
c. 2-bridge knot
d. -module

13. In mathematics, especially in the area of abstract algebra known as ring theory, a _____ is a ring with $0 \neq 1$ such that ab = 0 implies that either a = 0 or b = 0 (the zero-product property.) That is, it is a nontrivial ring without left or right zero divisors. A commutative _____ is called an integral _____.
a. Coherent ring
b. Subring
c. Partially-ordered ring
d. Domain

14. In mathematics, any vector space, V, has a corresponding dual vector space (or just dual space for short) consisting of all linear functionals on V. Dual vector spaces defined on finite-dimensional vector spaces can be used for defining tensors which are studied in tensor algebra. When applied to vector spaces of functions (which typically are infinite-dimensional), _____ are employed for defining and studying concepts like measures, distributions, and Hilbert spaces. Consequently, the dual space is an important concept in the study of functional analysis.
a. Jordan normal form
b. Barycentric coordinates
c. Conjugate transpose
d. Dual spaces

15. In ring theory, a branch of abstract algebra, an _____ is a special subset of a ring. The _____ concept generalizes in an appropriate way some important properties of integers like 'even number' or 'multiple of 3'.

Chapter 4. Goodies

For instance, in rings one studies prime ideals instead of prime numbers, one defines coprime ideals as a generalization of coprime numbers, and one can prove a generalized Chinese remainder theorem about ideals.

   a. ADE classification
   b. Augmentation ideal
   c. AKS primality test
   d. Ideal

16.   In ring theory, a branch of abstract algebra, a _____ is an ideal I in a ring R that is generated by a single element a of R.

More specifically:

- a left _____ of R is a subset of R of the form Ra := {ra : r in R};
- a right _____ is a subset of the form aR := {ar : r in R};
- a two-sided _____ is a subset of the form RaR := {$r_1 a s_1$ + ... + $r_n a s_n$: $r_1, s_1, ..., r_n, s_n$ in R}.

If R is a commutative ring, then the above three notions are all the same. In that case, it is common to write the ideal generated by a as (a.)

Not all ideals are principal.

   a. Primitive ideal
   b. Radical of an ring
   c. Radical of an ideal
   d. Principal ideal

17.   In abstract algebra, a _____ i.e., can be generated by a single element. More generally, a principal ring is a nonzero commutative ring whose ideals are principal, although some authors (e.g., Bourbaki) refers to Principal ideal domains as principal rings. The distinction being that a principal ideal ring may have zero divisors whereas a _____ cannot.
   a. Minimal prime
   b. Nilradical
   c. Discrete valuation
   d. Principal ideal domain

18.   In linear algebra, the quotient of a vector space V by a subspace N is a vector space obtained by 'collapsing' N to zero. The space obtained is called a _____ and is denoted V/N (read V mod N.)

Chapter 4. Goodies

a. Wedge sum
b. Smash product
c. Triangulation
d. Quotient space

19. In mathematics, there are several meanings of _____ depending on the subject.

A _____, usually denoted by ° (the _____ symbol), is a measurement of plane angle, representing $\frac{1}{360}$ of a full rotation. When that angle is with respect to a reference meridian, it indicates a location along a great circle of a sphere, such as Earth, Mars, or the celestial sphere.

a. Symmetric difference
b. Relation algebra
c. Median algebra
d. Degree

20. In abstract algebra, a _____ is an algebraic structure with notions of addition, subtraction, multiplication and division, satisfying certain axioms. The most commonly used fields are the _____ of real numbers, the _____ of complex numbers, and the _____ of rational numbers, but there are also finite fields, fields of functions, various algebraic number fields, p-adic fields, and so forth.

Any _____ may be used as the scalars for a vector space, which is the standard general context for linear algebra.

a. Tensor product of fields
b. Generic polynomial
c. Field
d. Separable

21. A _____ is a symbol that stands for a value that may vary; the term usually occurs in opposition to constant, which is a symbol for a non-varying value, i.e. completely fixed or fixed in the context of use. The concepts of constants and variables are fundamental to all modern mathematics, science, engineering, and computer programming.

Much of the basic theory for which we use variables today, such as school geometry and algebra, was developed thousands of years ago, but the use of symbolic formulae and variables is only several hundreds of years old.

a. -equivalence
b. -module
c. 2-bridge knot
d. Variable

22. In algebra, the _____ of a polynomial with real or complex coefficients is a certain expression in the coefficients of the polynomial which is a symmetric polynomial in the coefficients and gives information on the nature of the roots; in particular, it is equal to zero if and only if the polynomial has a multiple root (i.e. a root with multiplicity greater than one) in the complex numbers. For example, the _____ of the quadratic polynomial

$$ax^2 + bx + c \text{ is } b^2 - 4ac.$$

The _____ of the cubic polynomial

$$ax^3 + bx^2 + cx + d \text{ is } b^2c^2 - 4ac^3 - 4b^3d - 27a^2d^2 + 18abcd.$$

a. Polynomial remainder theorem
b. Minimal polynomial
c. Discriminant
d. Kazhdan-Lusztig polynomials

23. _____ or biquadratic reciprocity is a collection of theorems in elementary and algebraic number theory that state conditions under which the congruence $x^4 \equiv p \pmod{q}$ is solvable; the word 'reciprocity' comes from the form of some of these theorems, in that they relate the solvability of the congruence $x^4 \equiv p \pmod{q}$ to that of $x^4 \equiv q \pmod{p}$.

Euler made the first conjectures about biquadratic reciprocity. Gauss published two monographs on biquadratic reciprocity.

a. Cyclotomic character
b. Herbrand quotient
c. Modulus
d. Quartic

24. In abstract algebra, the _____ of a polynomial P(X) over a given field K is a field extension L of K, over which P factorizes into linear factors

$X - a_i,$

and such that the a_i generate L over K. It can be shown that such splitting fields exist, and are unique up to isomorphism; the amount of freedom in that isomorphism is known to be the Galois group of P.

For an example if K is the rational number field Q and

$$P = X^3 - 2,$$

then a _____ L will contain a primitive cube root of unity, as well as a cube root of 2. Thus

$$L = \mathbb{Q}(\sqrt[3]{2}, \omega_2) = \{a + b\omega_2 + c\sqrt[3]{2} + d\sqrt[3]{2}\omega_2 + e\sqrt[3]{2}^2 + f\sqrt[3]{2}^2\omega_2 \mid a,b,c,d,e,f \in \mathbb{Q}\}$$

where

$$\omega_1 = 1,$$
$$\omega_2 = -\frac{1}{2} + \frac{\sqrt{3}}{2}i,$$
$$\omega_3 = -\frac{1}{2} - \frac{\sqrt{3}}{2}i$$

, and

are the cubic roots of unity.

a. Splitting field
b. Fundamental theorem of Galois theory
c. Formally real field
d. Field of fractions

25. In mathematics, an _____ is an isomorphism from a mathematical object to itself. It is, in some sense, a symmetry of the object, and a way of mapping the object to itself while preserving all of its structure. The set of all automorphisms of an object forms a group, called the _____ group.
   a. Endomorphism
   b. ADE classification
   c. Automorphism
   d. Epimorphism

26. In mathematics, a _____ is a group associated with a certain type of field extension. The study of field extensions (and polynomials which give rise to them) via Galois groups is called Galois theory after Évariste Galois who first invented them

a. Field of fractions
b. Galois group
c. Splitting field
d. Primitive element theorem

27. A _____ is a set G closed under a binary operation · satisfying the following 3 axioms:

- Associativity: For all a, b and c in G, (a · b) · c = a · (b · c.)
- Identity element: There exists an e∈G such that for all a in G, e · a = a · e = a.
- Inverse element: For each a in G, there is an element b in G such that a · b = b · a = e, where e is an identity element.

Basic examples for groups are the integers Z with addition operation, or rational numbers without zero Q{0} with multiplication. More generally, for any ring R, the units in R form a multiplicative _____ Groups include, however, much more general structures than the above.

a. Nilpotent group
b. Grigorchuk group
c. Product of group subsets
d. Group

28. The _____ of a Lie algebra $\mathfrak{g}$ is a particular ideal of $\mathfrak{g}$.

Let $\mathfrak{g}$ be a Lie algebra. The _____ of $\mathfrak{g}$ is defined as the largest solvable ideal of $\mathfrak{g}$.

a. Cyclically reduced word
b. Radical
c. Garside element
d. Class sum

29. In algebra, _____ is one of the cases that may arise in attempting to solve a cubic equation with integer coefficients with roots that are expressed with radicals. Specifically, if a cubic polynomial is irreducible over the rational numbers and has three real roots, then in order to express the roots with radicals, one must introduce complex-valued expressions, even though the resulting expressions are ultimately real-valued. _____ was the original reason for the introduction of the complex number system by Niccolò Fontana Tartaglia and Gerolamo Cardano in 1545.

a. Birational invariant
b. Casus irreducibilis
c. Tight closure
d. Reduced ring

Chapter 5. Groups II

1. In abstract algebra, the _____ is a construction which combines several modules into a new, larger module. The result of the direct summation of modules is the 'smallest general' module which contains the given modules as subspaces. This is an example of a coproduct.

    a. Finite dimensional von Neumann algebra
    b. Schmidt decomposition
    c. Direct sum
    d. Frame

2. An _____ is a group satisfying the requirement that the result of applying the group operation to two group elements does not depend on their order Abelian groups generalize the arithmetic of addition of integers; they are named after Niels Henrik Abel.

    The concept of an _____ is one of the first concepts encountered in undergraduate abstract algebra, with many other basic objects, such as a module and a vector space, being its refinements.

    a. Algebraically compact
    b. ADE classification
    c. Elementary abelian group
    d. Abelian group

3. In mathematics, in the field of group theory, a _____ of a finite group is a quasisimple subnormal subgroup. Any two distinct components commute. The product of all the components is the layer of the group.

    a. Group homomorphism
    b. Wreath product
    c. Stallings' theorem about ends of groups
    d. Component

4. A _____ is a set G closed under a binary operation · satisfying the following 3 axioms:

    - Associativity: For all a, b and c in G, (a · b) · c = a · (b · c.)
    - Identity element: There exists an e∈G such that for all a in G, e · a = a · e = a.
    - Inverse element: For each a in G, there is an element b in G such that a · b = b · a = e, where e is an identity element.

    Basic examples for groups are the integers Z with addition operation, or rational numbers without zero Q{0} with multiplication. More generally, for any ring R, the units in R form a multiplicative _____ Groups include, however, much more general structures than the above.

Chapter 5. Groups II

  a. Grigorchuk group
  b. Nilpotent group
  c. Group
  d. Product of group subsets

5. A _____ is an n × n table filled with n different symbols in such a way that each symbol occurs exactly once in each row and exactly once in each column. Here is an example: $\begin{bmatrix} 1 & 2 & 3 \\ 2 & 3 & 1 \\ 3 & 1 & 2 \end{bmatrix}$

Latin squares occur as the multiplication tables of quasigroups. They have applications in the design of experiments and in error correcting codes.

  a. 2-bridge knot
  b. Latin square
  c. -equivalence
  d. -module

6. In mathematics, especially in the area of algebra studying the theory of abelian groups, a _____ is a generalization of direct summand. It has found many uses in abelian group theory and related areas.

A subgroup S of a (typically abelian) group G is said to be pure if whenever an element of S has an nth root in G, it necessarily has an nth root in S.

  a. -equivalence
  b. -module
  c. 2-bridge knot
  d. Pure subgroup

7. In linear algebra, a _____ is a set of vectors that, in a linear combination, can represent every vector in a given vector space or free module, and such that no element of the set can be represented as a linear combination of the others. In other words, a _____ is a linearly independent spanning set.
  a. Minor
  b. Chirality
  c. Basis
  d. Supergroup

8. In algebraic geometry, divisors are a generalization of codimension one subvarieties of algebraic varieties; two different generalizations are in common use, Cartier divisors and Weil divisors The concepts agree on non-singular varieties over algebraically closed fields.

A Weil _____ is a locally finite linear combination (with integral coefficients) of irreducible subvarieties of codimension one.

   a. Lefschetz pencil
   b. Picard group
   c. Linear system of divisors
   d. Divisor

9. In algebra, the _____ of a module over a principal ideal domain occur in one form of the structure theorem for finitely generated modules over a principal ideal domain.

If R is a PID and M a finitely generated R-module, then M is isomorphic to a unique sum of the form

$$M \cong R^r \oplus \bigoplus_i R/(q_i)$$

where $q_i \neq 1$ and the (q_i) are primary ideals.

The ideals (q_i) are unique (up to order); the elements q_i are unique up to associatedness, and are called the _____.

   a. Invariant factors
   b. Extension of scalars
   c. Injective hull
   d. Elementary divisors

10. In abstract algebra, the term _____ refers to a number of concepts related to elements of finite order in groups and to the failure of modules to be free.

Let G be a group. An element g of G is called a _____ element if g has finite order.

   a. Divisible group
   b. Torsion subgroup
   c. Cyclic group
   d. Torsion

Chapter 5. Groups II

11. In the theory of abelian groups, the _____ A_T of an abelian group A is the subgroup of A consisting of all elements that have finite order. An abelian group A is called a torsion (or periodic) group if every element of A has finite order and is called torsion-free if every element of A except the identity is of infinite order.

The proof that A_T is closed under addition relies on the commutativity of addition

   a. Cyclic group
   b. Locally cyclic group
   c. Divisible group
   d. Torsion subgroup

12. In abstract algebra, a _____ provides a way to break up an algebraic structure, such as a group or a module, into simple pieces. The need for considering _____ in the context of modules arises from the fact that many naturally occurring modules are not semisimple, hence cannot be decomposed into a direct sum of simple modules. A _____ of a module M is a finite increasing filtration of M by submodules such that the successive quotients are simple and serves as a replacement of the direct sum decomposition of M into its simple constituents.

   a. Burnside's theorem
   b. Baby-step giant-step
   c. Composition series
   d. Conjugacy class

13. In algebra, a commutative ring R is said to be _____ if any of the following equivalent conditions holds:

   1. The localization $R_\mathfrak{m}$ of R at $\mathfrak{m}$ is a valuation ring for every maximal ideal $\mathfrak{m}$ of R.
   2. For all ideals $\mathfrak{a}, \mathfrak{b}$, and $\mathfrak{c}$,

   $$\mathfrak{a} \cap (\mathfrak{b} + \mathfrak{c}) = (\mathfrak{a} \cap \mathfrak{b}) + (\mathfrak{a} \cap \mathfrak{c})$$

   - For all ideals $\mathfrak{a}, \mathfrak{b}$, and $\mathfrak{c}$,

   $$\mathfrak{a} + (\mathfrak{b} \cap \mathfrak{c}) = (\mathfrak{a} + \mathfrak{b}) \cap (\mathfrak{a} + \mathfrak{c})$$

An _____ domain is called a Prüfer domain.

   a. Exchange matrix
   b. Ordered vector space
   c. Inverse eigenvalues theorem
   d. Arithmetical

Chapter 5. Groups II

14. In mathematics, the _____ gives an indication of the extent to which a certain binary operation fails to be commutative. There are different definitions used in group theory and ring theory.

The _____ of two elements, g and h, of a group, G, is the element

$$[g, h] = g^{-1}h^{-1}gh$$

It is equal to the group's identity if and only if g and h commute (i.e., if and only if gh = hg.)

   a. Dimension theorem for vector spaces
   b. Linear combinations
   c. Coimage
   d. Commutator

15. In mathematics, there are several meanings of _____ depending on the subject.

A _____, usually denoted by ° (the _____ symbol), is a measurement of plane angle, representing $\frac{1}{360}$ of a full rotation. When that angle is with respect to a reference meridian, it indicates a location along a great circle of a sphere, such as Earth, Mars, or the celestial sphere.

   a. Symmetric difference
   b. Median algebra
   c. Relation algebra
   d. Degree

16. A _____ is a symbol that stands for a value that may vary; the term usually occurs in opposition to constant, which is a symbol for a non-varying value, i.e. completely fixed or fixed in the context of use. The concepts of constants and variables are fundamental to all modern mathematics, science, engineering, and computer programming.

Much of the basic theory for which we use variables today, such as school geometry and algebra, was developed thousands of years ago, but the use of symbolic formulae and variables is only several hundreds of years old.

   a. 2-bridge knot
   b. -equivalence
   c. Variable
   d. -module

Chapter 5. Groups II

17. A _____ is a complex number whose real and imaginary part are both integers. The Gaussian integers, with ordinary addition and multiplication of complex numbers, form an integral domain, usually written as Z[i]. This domain does not have a total ordering that respects arithmetic, since it contains imaginary numbers.
   a. Quadratic Gauss sums
   b. Kummer sum
   c. Jacobi sum
   d. Gaussian integer

18. The group (Z,+) of integers is free; we can take S = {1}. A _____ on a two-element set S occurs in the proof of the Banach-Tarski paradox and is described there.

   On the other hand, any nontrivial finite group cannot be free, since the elements of a free generating set of a _____ have infinite order.

   a. Baby-step giant-step
   b. Fitting length
   c. Class function
   d. Free group

19. The _____ are natural numbers including 0 ' href='/wiki/0_(number)'>0, 1, 2, 3, ...) and their negatives (0, −1, −2, −3, ...). They are numbers that can be written without a fractional or decimal component, and fall within the set {...
   a. ADE classification
   b. Abelian P-root group
   c. AKS primality test
   d. Integers

20. _____, in mathematics, are a non-commutative number system that extends the complex numbers. The _____ were first described by Irish mathematician Sir William Rowan Hamilton in 1843 and applied to mechanics in three-dimensional space. They find uses in both theoretical and applied mathematics, in particular for calculations involving three-dimensional rotations , such as in 3D computer graphics, although they have been superseded in many applications by vectors and matrices.
   a. Split-quaternions
   b. Split-biquaternion
   c. Generalized quaternion interpolation
   d. Quaternions

Chapter 5. Groups II

21. In abstract algebra, the _____ of a module is a measure of the module's 'size'. It is defined as the _____ of the longest ascending chain of submodules and is a generalization of the concept of dimension for vector spaces. The modules with finite _____ share many important properties with finite-dimensional vector spaces.

   a. Length
   b. Supermodule
   c. Finitely generated module
   d. Morita equivalence

22. A _____ between two algebras over a field K, A and B, is a map $F : A \to B$ such that for all k in K and x,y in A,

   - F(kx) = kF(x)
   - F(x + y) = F(x) + F(y)
   - F(xy) = F(x)F(y)

   If F is bijective then F is said to be an isomorphism between A and B.

   Let A = K[x] be the set of all polynomials over a field K and B be the set of all polynomial functions over K. Both A and B are algebras over K given by the standard multiplication and addition of polynomials and functions, respectively. We can map each f in A to $\hat{f}$ in B by the rule $\hat{f}(t) = f(t)$. A routine check shows that the mapping $f \mapsto \hat{f}$ is a _____ of the algebras A and B. If K is a finite field then let

   $$p(x) = \Pi_{t \in K}(x - t).$$

   p is a nonzero polynomial in K[x], however $p(t) = 0$ for all t in K, so $\hat{p} = 0$ is the zero function and the algebras are not isomorphic.

   a. Tensor product of algebras
   b. Tensor algebra
   c. Frobenius matrix
   d. Homomorphism

23. In abstract algebra, a branch of mathematics, a _____ is an algebraic structure with a single, associative binary operation and an identity element. Monoids occur in a number of branches of mathematics and capture the idea of function composition; indeed, this notion is abstracted in category theory, where the _____ is a category with one object. Monoids are also commonly used to provide an algebraic foundation for computer science; in this case, the transition _____ and syntactic _____ are used in describing a finite state machine, whereas trace monoids and history monoids provide a foundation for process calculi and concurrent computing.

a. Rupture field
b. Monoid
c. Goodman-Nguyen-van Fraassen algebra
d. Precedence rule

24. In mathematics, a _____ is an algebraic structure consisting of a nonempty set S together with an associative binary operation. In other words, a _____ is an associative magma. The terminology is derived from the anterior notion of a group.
a. Syndetic set
b. Regular semigroup
c. Free monoid
d. Semigroup

25. In mathematics, one method of defining a group is by a _____. One specifies a set S of generators so that every element of the group can be written as a product of some of these generators, and a set R of relations among those generators. We then say G has _____

$$\langle S \mid R \rangle.$$

Informally, G has the above _____ if it is the 'freest group' generated by S subject only to the relations R. Formally, the group G is said to have the above _____ if it is isomorphic to the quotient of a free group on S by the normal subgroup generated by the relations R.

a. -equivalence
b. Tietze transformations
c. -module
d. Presentation

Chapter 6. Commutative Rings II

1. In mathematics, a _____ is a type of algebraic structure. There is some variation among mathematicians as to exactly what properties a _____ is required to have, as described in detail below. However, commonly a _____ is defined as a set together with two binary operations (usually called addition and multiplication), where each operation combines two elements to form a third element.

   a. -equivalence
   b. -module
   c. Ring
   d. 2-bridge knot

2. In ring theory, a branch of abstract algebra, an _____ is a special subset of a ring. The _____ concept generalizes in an appropriate way some important properties of integers like 'even number' or 'multiple of 3'.

   For instance, in rings one studies prime ideals instead of prime numbers, one defines coprime ideals as a generalization of coprime numbers, and one can prove a generalized Chinese remainder theorem about ideals.

   a. Augmentation ideal
   b. AKS primality test
   c. ADE classification
   d. Ideal

3. In mathematics, a _____ is a subset of a ring which shares many important properties of a prime number in the ring of integers Prime ideals in order theory are treated in the article on ideals in order theory.

   a. Radical of an ring
   b. Principal ideal
   c. Prime ideal
   d. Radical of an ideal

4. In mathematics, more specifically in ring theory, a _____ is an ideal which is maximal (with respect to set inclusion) amongst all proper ideals, i.e. which is not contained in any other proper ideal of the ring.

   Maximal ideals are important because the quotient rings of maximal ideals are simple rings, and in the special case of unital commutative rings they are also fields. Rings which contain only one _____ are called local rings.

   a. Principal ideal
   b. Jacobson radical
   c. Radical of an ring
   d. Maximal ideal

5. The _____ is a result about congruences in number theory and its generalizations in abstract algebra.

Chapter 6. Commutative Rings II

The original form of the theorem, contained in a third-century AD book Sun Zi suanjing by Chinese mathematician Sun Tzu and later republished in a 1247 book by Qin Jiushao, the Shushu Jiuzhang (æ•¸æ›¸ä¹ ç« Mathematical Treatise in Nine Sections) is a statement about simultaneous congruences

Suppose n_1, n_2, â€¦, n_k are positive integers which are pairwise coprime.

a. Multiplicative group of integers modulo n
b. Discrete logarithm
c. Modular arithmetic
d. Chinese Remainder Theorem

6. In ring theory, a branch of abstract algebra, a _____ is a ring in which the multiplication operation is commutative. The study of commutative rings is called commutative algebra.

Some specific kinds of commutative rings are given with the following chain of class inclusions:

- commutative rings ⊃ integral domains ⊃ unique factorization domains ⊃ principal ideal domains ⊃ Euclidean domains ⊃ fields

A ring is a set R equipped with two binary operations, i.e. operations that combine any two elements of the ring to a third. They are called addition and multiplication and commonly denoted by '+' and '·', e.g. a + b and a · b.

a. Differential calculus over commutative algebras
b. Going up
c. Nilradical
d. Commutative ring

7. In mathematics, especially in the area of abstract algebra known as ring theory, a _____ is a ring with 0 ≠ 1 such that ab = 0 implies that either a = 0 or b = 0 (the zero-product property.) That is, it is a nontrivial ring without left or right zero divisors. A commutative _____ is called an integral _____.
a. Subring
b. Coherent ring
c. Partially-ordered ring
d. Domain

8. In mathematics, _____ or factoring is the decomposition of an object ' href='/wiki/Matrix_(mathematics)'>matrix) into a product of other objects, or factors, which when multiplied together give the original. For example, the number 15 factors into primes as 3 × 5, and the polynomial $x^2 - 4$ factors as $(x - 2)(x + 2)$. In all cases, a product of simpler objects is obtained.

   a. 2-bridge knot
   b. -equivalence
   c. -module
   d. Factorization

9. In mathematics, a _____ is, roughly speaking, a commutative ring in which every element, with special exceptions, can be uniquely written as a product of prime elements, analogous to the fundamental theorem of arithmetic for the integers. Unique factorization domains are sometimes called factorial rings, following the terminology of Bourbaki.

Note that unique factorization domains appear in the following chain of class inclusions:

- Commutative rings >⊃ integral domains >⊃ unique factorization domains >⊃ principal ideal domains >⊃ Euclidean domains >⊃ fields

   a. Unit ring
   b. Isomorphism class
   c. Absorption law
   d. Unique factorization domain

10. In algebraic geometry, divisors are a generalization of codimension one subvarieties of algebraic varieties; two different generalizations are in common use, Cartier divisors and Weil divisors The concepts agree on non-singular varieties over algebraically closed fields.

A Weil _____ is a locally finite linear combination (with integral coefficients) of irreducible subvarieties of codimension one.

   a. Divisor
   b. Lefschetz pencil
   c. Picard group
   d. Linear system of divisors

11. A _____ is a complex number whose real and imaginary part are both integers. The Gaussian integers, with ordinary addition and multiplication of complex numbers, form an integral domain, usually written as Z[i]. This domain does not have a total ordering that respects arithmetic, since it contains imaginary numbers.

a. Jacobi sum
b. Quadratic Gauss sums
c. Kummer sum
d. Gaussian integer

12. The _____ are natural numbers including 0 ' href='/wiki/0_(number)'>0, 1, 2, 3, ...) and their negatives (0, −1, −2, −3, ...). They are numbers that can be written without a fractional or decimal component, and fall within the set {...

a. Abelian P-root group
b. ADE classification
c. AKS primality test
d. Integers

13. In field theory, a branch of mathematics, a _____ is the minimal polynomial of a primitive element of the finite extension field GF(p^m.) In other words, a polynomial F(X) with coefficients in GF(p) = Z/pZ is a _____ if it has a root α in GF(p^m) such that $\{0, 1, \alpha, \alpha^2, \alpha^3, \ldots, \alpha^{p^m-2}\}$ is the entire field GF(p^m), and moreover, F(X) is the smallest degree polynomial having α as root.

In ring theory, the term _____ is used for a different purpose, to mean a polynomial over a unique factorization domain (such as the integers) whose greatest common divisor of its coefficients is a unit.

a. Kummer theory
b. Separable
c. Primitive polynomial
d. Formally real field

14. In algebra, the _____ of a polynomial is the highest common factor of its coefficients.

A polynomial is primitive if it has _____ unity.

Gauss's lemma for polynomials may be expressed as stating that for polynomials over a unique factorization domain, the _____ of the product of two polynomials is the product of their contents.

a. Permanent
b. Filtration
c. Nested radical
d. Content

Chapter 6. Commutative Rings II

15. The _____ and descending chain condition (DCC) are finiteness properties satisfied by certain algebraic structures, most importantly, ideals in a commutative ring. These conditions played an important role in the development of the structure theory of commutative rings in the works of David Hilbert, Emmy Noether, and Emil Artin. The conditions themselves can be stated in an abstract form, so that they make sense for any partially ordered set.
   a. Invariant polynomial
   b. Integral
   c. Atomic domain
   d. Ascending chain condition

16. In algebraic topology, a simplicial k-_____ is a formal linear combination of k-simplices.

Integration is defined on chains by taking the linear combination of integrals over the simplices in the _____ with coefficients typically integers. The set of all k-chains forms a group and the sequence of these groups is called a _____ complex.

   a. Combinatorial topology
   b. Bockstein homomorphism
   c. Tesseract
   d. Chain

17. In linear algebra, a _____ is a set of vectors that, in a linear combination, can represent every vector in a given vector space or free module, and such that no element of the set can be represented as a linear combination of the others. In other words, a _____ is a linearly independent spanning set.
   a. Supergroup
   b. Chirality
   c. Minor
   d. Basis

18. In mathematics, an _____ is an algebraic structure consisting of a vector space together with an operation, usually called multiplication, that combines any two vectors to form a third vector. To qualify as an algebra, the multiplication must satisfy certain compatibility axioms with the given vector space structure, such as distributivity. In other words, an _____ is a set together with operations of multiplication, addition, and scalar multiplication by elements of the field.
   a. Alternant matrix
   b. Artin-Rees lemma
   c. Imperfect group
   d. Algebra over a field

Chapter 6. Commutative Rings II

19. In abstract algebra, a _____ is an algebraic structure with notions of addition, subtraction, multiplication and division, satisfying certain axioms. The most commonly used fields are the _____ of real numbers, the _____ of complex numbers, and the _____ of rational numbers, but there are also finite fields, fields of functions, various algebraic number fields, p-adic fields, and so forth.

Any _____ may be used as the scalars for a vector space, which is the standard general context for linear algebra.

a. Tensor product of fields
b. Field
c. Generic polynomial
d. Separable

20. A _____ is a symbol that stands for a value that may vary; the term usually occurs in opposition to constant, which is a symbol for a non-varying value, i.e. completely fixed or fixed in the context of use. The concepts of constants and variables are fundamental to all modern mathematics, science, engineering, and computer programming.

Much of the basic theory for which we use variables today, such as school geometry and algebra, was developed thousands of years ago, but the use of symbolic formulae and variables is only several hundreds of years old.

a. Variable
b. -equivalence
c. 2-bridge knot
d. -module

21. In mathematics, namely algebraic geometry, the _____ is a particular topology chosen for algebraic varieties that reflects the algebraic nature of their definition. It is due to Oscar Zariski and took a place of particular importance in the field around 1950. Joe Harris says in his introductory lectures that it is 'not a real topology' and points out that in the _____, every two algebraic curves are homeomorphic simply because their underlying sets have equal cardinalities and their topologies are both cofinite.

a. Segre embedding
b. Theorem of the cube
c. Degree of an algebraic variety
d. Zariski topology

22. In mathematics, an element x of a ring R is called _____ if there exists some positive integer n such that $x^n = 0$.

The term was introduced by Benjamin Peirce in the context of elements of an algebra that vanish when raised to a power.

- This definition can be applied in particular to square matrices. The matrix

$$A = \begin{pmatrix} 0 & 1 & 0 \\ 0 & 0 & 1 \\ 0 & 0 & 0 \end{pmatrix}$$

is _____ because $A^3 = 0$. See _____ matrix for more.

a. Ring of integers
b. Hochschild homology
c. Product ring
d. Nilpotent

23. The _____ of a Lie algebra $\mathfrak{g}$ is a particular ideal of $\mathfrak{g}$.

Let $\mathfrak{g}$ be a Lie algebra. The _____ of $\mathfrak{g}$ is defined as the largest solvable ideal of $\mathfrak{g}$.

a. Cyclically reduced word
b. Radical
c. Garside element
d. Class sum

24. In mathematics, the adjective _____ means that an object cannot be expressed as a product of more than one non-trivial factors in a given set. See also factorization.

For any field F, the ring of polynomials with coefficients in F is denoted by F[x].

a. Irreducible
b. Integer-valued polynomial
c. Ehrhart polynomial
d. Alternating polynomial

Chapter 6. Commutative Rings II

25. In set theory, the term _____ refers to a set operation used in the convergence of set elements to form a resultant set containing the elements of both sets. As a simple example, a _____ of two disjoint sets, which do not have elements in common results in a set containing all elements from both sets. A Venn diagram representing the _____ of sets A and B. If one circle represents A, and the other B, then the red area represents the _____ of A and B. The area where the circles join, also shown in red, is the intersection of the two sets.

If we define two sets which contain unique elements; those of A not occurring in B and vice versa, then the _____ of these sets results in a set which contains all elements of A and B. In terms of notation, we could define this set operation as the following:

A = {1,2,3,4}
B = {5,6,7,8}
$$A \cup B = \{1, 2, 3, 4, 5, 6, 7, 8\}$$

Other more complex operations can be done including the _____, if the set is for example defined by a property rather than a finite or assumed infinite enumeration of elements.

a. AKS primality test
b. ADE classification
c. Abelian P-root group
d. Union

26. In mathematics, the _____ of two sets A and B is the set that contains all elements of A that also belong to B (or equivalently, all elements of B that also belong to A), but no other elements.

For explanation of the symbols used in this article, refer to the table of mathematical symbols.

The _____ of A and B

The _____ of A and B is written 'A ∩ B'.

a. AKS primality test
b. Intersection
c. Abelian P-root group
d. ADE classification

27. In algebra, the _____ of a commutative ring is a nilpotent ideal, which is as large as possible. In the non-commutative ring case, more care is needed resulting in several related radicals.

The _____ of a commutative ring is the set of all nilpotent elements in the ring, or equivalently the radical of the zero ideal.

Chapter 6. Commutative Rings II

a. Noether normalization lemma
b. Nilradical
c. Top
d. Hilbert polynomial

28. In mathematics, there are several meanings of _____ depending on the subject.

A _____, usually denoted by ° (the _____ symbol), is a measurement of plane angle, representing $\frac{1}{360}$ of a full rotation. When that angle is with respect to a reference meridian, it indicates a location along a great circle of a sphere, such as Earth, Mars, or the celestial sphere.

a. Symmetric difference
b. Relation algebra
c. Degree
d. Median algebra

29. In mathematics, the word _____ means two different things in the context of polynomials:

- The first meaning is a product of powers of variables, or formally any value obtained from 1 by finitely many multiplications by a variable. If only a single variable x is considered this means that any _____ is either 1 or a power x^n of x, with n a positive integer. If several variables are considered, say, x, y, z, then each can be given an exponent, so that any _____ is of the form $x^a y^b z^c$ with a,b,c nonnegative integers (taking note that any exponent 0 makes the corresponding factor equal to 1.)
- The second meaning of _____ includes monomials in the first sense, but also allows multiplication by any constant, so that $-7x^5$ and $(3 - 4i)x^4 yz^{13}$ are also considered to be monomials (the second example assuming polynomials in x, y, z over the complex numbers are considered.)

With either definition, the set of monomials is a subset of all polynomials that is closed under multiplication.

Both uses of this notion can be found, and in many cases the distinction is simply ignored, see for instance examples for the first and second meaning, and an unclear definition. In informal discussions the distinction is seldom important, and tendency is towards the broader second meaning. When studying the structure of polynomials however, one often definitely needs a notion with the first meaning.

a. Diagonal form
b. Schur polynomials
c. Power sum symmetric polynomial
d. Monomial

Chapter 6. Commutative Rings II

30. In mathematics, a _____ is a total order on the set of all monomials (considering monomials which only differ in their coefficient to be the same) satisfying two additional properties.

   1. If u < v and w is any other monomial, then uw<vw. In other words, the ordering respects multiplication.
   2. The ordering is a well ordering

Most monomial orders impose an ordering on the indeterminates, but differ in their exact details. Some important examples of monomial orders include:

- Lexicographic order (lex) orders according to the highest power of the most significant indeterminate, using less significant indeterminates to break ties.

- Reverse lexicographic order (revlex) orders according to the lowest power of the least significant indeterminate, using more significant indeterminates to break ties.

- Graded lexicographic order (grlex) orders by total degree first, then breaks ties using lexicographic order.

- Graded reverse lexicographic order (grevlex) orders by total degree first, then breaks ties using reverse lexicographic order.

- An elimination order guarantees that a monomial involving any of a set of indeterminates will always be greater than a monomial not involving any of them.

- A product order orders one set of indeterminates using one _____, then breaks ties using a different order on a second set.

- Weight orders treat the powers of indeterminates as a vector and orders according to the dot product with a weight vector.

All monomial orders can be constructed as product orders of weight orders (Cox et al. pp.

   a. -equivalence
   b. -module
   c. 2-bridge knot
   d. Monomial order

31. In group theory, a branch of mathematics, the term _____ is used in two closely related senses:

- the _____ of a group is its cardinality, i.e. the number of its elements;
- the _____, sometimes period, of an element a of a group is the smallest positive integer m such that a^m = e (where e denotes the identity element of the group, and a^m denotes the product of m copies of a.) If no such m exists, we say that a has infinite _____. All elements of finite groups have finite _____.

We denote the _____ of a group G by ord(G) or |G| and the _____ of an element a by ord(a) or |a|.

Example. The symmetric group S_3 has the following multiplication table.

This group has six elements, so ord(S_3) = 6.

a. Outer automorphism group
b. Index calculus algorithm
c. Artin group
d. Order

32. In mathematics, _____ refers to the rewriting of an expression into a simpler form. For example, the process of rewriting a fraction into one with the smallest whole-number denominator possible (while keeping the numerator an integer) is called 'reducing a fraction'. Rewriting a radical (or 'root') expression with the smallest possible whole number under the radical symbol is called 'reducing a radical'.
  a. -module
  b. Reduction
  c. 2-bridge knot
  d. -equivalence

ANSWER KEY

Chapter 1
1. c   2. b   3. d   4. d   5. d   6. c   7. d   8. a   9. d   10. a
11. d   12. d   13. d   14. b   15. b   16. d   17. d   18. c   19. d   20. d
21. d   22. c   23. a   24. b   25. c   26. b   27. d   28. d   29. d   30. d
31. d   32. c   33. d   34. d

Chapter 2
1. b   2. d   3. d   4. d   5. c   6. b   7. d   8. c   9. d   10. d
11. d   12. a   13. d   14. a   15. d   16. a   17. d   18. d   19. c   20. a
21. d   22. a   23. d   24. d   25. a   26. b   27. d   28. d   29. d   30. a
31. a   32. d   33. a   34. d   35. d   36. b   37. d   38. d   39. d   40. d
41. d   42. d   43. d   44. a   45. d   46. d   47. b   48. c

Chapter 3
1. b   2. c   3. b   4. a   5. b   6. d   7. b   8. d   9. d   10. d
11. d   12. d   13. b   14. c   15. d   16. d   17. d   18. d   19. d   20. a
21. b   22. d   23. b   24. a   25. a   26. d   27. d   28. b   29. d   30. b
31. a   32. d   33. d   34. d   35. d   36. b   37. d   38. b   39. c   40. d
41. d   42. d   43. d   44. d   45. c   46. d   47. a   48. a   49. a   50. c
51. b   52. d   53. d   54. d

Chapter 4
1. c   2. d   3. c   4. a   5. d   6. c   7. a   8. a   9. c   10. b
11. b   12. b   13. d   14. d   15. d   16. d   17. d   18. d   19. d   20. c
21. d   22. c   23. d   24. a   25. c   26. b   27. d   28. b   29. b

Chapter 5
1. c   2. d   3. d   4. c   5. b   6. d   7. c   8. d   9. d   10. d
11. d   12. c   13. d   14. d   15. d   16. c   17. d   18. d   19. d   20. d
21. a   22. d   23. b   24. d   25. d

Chapter 6
1. c   2. d   3. c   4. d   5. d   6. d   7. d   8. d   9. d   10. a
11. d   12. d   13. c   14. d   15. d   16. d   17. d   18. d   19. b   20. a
21. d   22. d   23. b   24. a   25. d   26. b   27. b   28. c   29. d   30. d
31. d   32. b

www.ingramcontent.com/pod-product-compliance
Lightning Source LLC
Chambersburg PA
CBHW081848230426
43669CB00018B/2873